THE WAY
PEOPLE
LIVE

Life on the Underground Railroad

Titles in The Way People Live series include:

Life on the Underground Railroad

by Stuart A. Kallen

Lucent Books, P.O. Box 289011, San Diego, CA 92198-9011

Library of Congress Cataloging-in-Publication Data

Kallen, Stuart A., 1955–
    Life on the Underground Railroad / by Stuart A. Kallen.
        p.   cm. — (The way people live)
    Includes bibliographical references (p.   ) and index.
    Summary: Describes what it was like to be involved in the Underground
Railroad, discussing life on the run, the lives of the trackers, conductors, and
stationmasters, and the building of new lives in Canada.
    ISBN 1-56006-667-9 (lib. bdg. : alk. paper)
    1. Underground railroad—Juvenile literature.   2. Fugitive slaves—
United States—Juvenile literature.   [1. Underground railroad. 2. Fugitive
slaves.] I. Title. II. Series.
    E450.K26   2000
    973.7'115—dc21   99-37101
                                                                                          CIP

Copyright 2000 by Lucent Books, Inc., P.O. Box 289011, San Diego, California
92198-9011

Printed in the U.S.A.

Contents

Discovering the Humanity in Us All

Books in The Way People Live series focus on groups of people in a wide variety of circumstances, settings, and time periods. Some books focus on different cultural groups, others, on people in a particular historical time period, while others cover people involved in a specific event. Each book emphasizes the daily routines, personal and historical struggles, and achievements of people from all walks of life.

To really understand any culture, it is necessary to strip the mind of the common notions we hold about groups of people. These stereotypes are the archenemies of learning. It does not even matter whether the stereotypes are positive or negative; they are confining and tight. Removing them is a challenge that's not easily met, as anyone who has ever tried it will admit. Ideas that do not fit into the templates we create are unwelcome visitors—ones we would prefer remain quietly in a corner or forgotten room.

The cowboy of the Old West is a good example of such confining roles. The cowboy was courageous, yet soft-spoken. His time (it is always a he, in our template) was spent alternatively saving a rancher's daughter from certain death on a runaway stagecoach, or shooting it out with rustlers. At times, of course, he was likely to get a little crazy in town after a trail drive, but for the most part, he was the epitome of inner strength. It is disconcerting to find out that the cowboy is human, even a bit childish. Can it really be true that cowboys would line up to help the cook on the trail drive grind coffee, just hoping he would give them a little stick of peppermint candy that came with the coffee shipment? The idea of tough cowboys vying with one another to help "Coosie" (as they called their cooks) for a bit of candy seems silly and out of place.

So is the vision of Eskimos playing video games and watching MTV, living in prefab housing in the Arctic. It just does not fit with what "Eskimo" means. We are far more comfortable with snow igloos and whale blubber, harpoons and kayaks.

Although the cultures dealt with in Lucent's The Way People Live series are often historically and socially well known, the emphasis is on the personal aspects of life. Groups of people, while unquestionably affected by their politics and their governmental structures, are more than those institutions. How do people in a particular time and place educate their children? What do they eat? And how do they build their houses? What kinds of work do they do? What kinds of games do they enjoy? The answers to these questions bring these cultures to life. People's lives are revealed in the particulars and only by knowing the particulars can we understand these cultures' will to survive and their moments of weakness and greatness.

This is not to say that understanding politics does not help to understand a culture. There is no question that the Warsaw ghetto, for example, was a culture that was brought about by the politics and social ideas of Adolf

Hitler and the Third Reich. But the Jews who were crowded together in the ghetto cannot be understood by the Reich's politics. Their life was a day-to-day battle for existence, and the creativity and methods they used to prolong their lives is a vital story of human perseverance that would be denied by focusing only on the institutions of Hitler's Germany. Knowing that children as young as five or six outwitted Nazi guards on a daily basis, that Jewish policemen helped the Germans control the ghetto, that children attended secret schools in the ghetto and even earned diplomas—these are the things that reveal the fabric of life, that can inspire, intrigue, and amaze.

Books in The Way People Live series allow both the casual reader and the student to see humans as victims, heroes, and onlookers. And although humans act in ways that can fill us with feelings of sorrow and revulsion, it is important to remember that "hero," "predator," and "victim" are dangerous terms. Heaping undue pity or praise on people reduces them to objects, and strips them of their humanity.

Seeing the Jews of Warsaw only as victims is to deny their humanity. Seeing them only as they appear in surviving photos, staring at the camera with infinite sadness, is limiting, both to them and to those who want to understand them. To an object of pity, the only appropriate response becomes "Those poor creatures!" and that reduces both the quality of their struggle and the depth of their despair. No one is served by such two-dimensional views of people and their cultures.

With this in mind, The Way People Live series strives to flesh out the traditional, two-dimensional views of people in various cultures and historical circumstances. Using a wide variety of primary quotations—the words not only of the politicians and government leaders, but of the real people whose lives are being examined—each book in the series attempts to show an honest and complete picture of a culture removed from our own by time or space.

By examining cultures in this way, the reader will notice not only the glaring differences from his or her own culture, but also will be struck by the similarities. For indeed, people share common needs—warmth, good company, stability, and affirmation from others. Ultimately, seeing how people really live, or have lived, can only enrich our understanding of ourselves.

The Long Road to Freedom

Slavery is as old as human history. The first tablets of writing made six thousand years ago in Sumer (modern-day Iraq) mention slavery—the practice of one person forcing another to work for no compensation. And slavery has appeared almost universally throughout history, from the slaves who built the great pyramids in ancient Egypt to the slaves who worked the plantations in the southern United States in the nineteenth century.

In Africa, slavery had been a common practice among tribes for centuries. Slaves were usually taken in war raids and were used to enhance the power of tribal chiefs. When Europeans first arrived on the African coast in the fifteenth century, chiefs were willing to bargain their human wealth for gunpowder, weapons, liquor, and cloth. The slave traders took only the youngest and strongest men and women because they had a better chance of surviving the horrid conditions aboard the ships.

Over the course of the next four hundred years, the slave trade was practiced by the Portuguese, Dutch, British, Spanish, and French. It was a lucrative business: Slaves that were purchased in Africa for about $25 sold for as much as $200 in the New World. (In 1808, it became illegal to import slaves from Africa to the United States, and the price of slaves skyrocketed to as much as $2,500.)

The first slaves arrived in the British North American colonies in 1619 when a Dutch vessel brought twenty Africans to Jamestown, Virginia, where they were traded for food. The number of slaves brought to North America multiplied yearly, and by 1708 there were twelve thousand African Americans in Virginia, compared with eighteen thousand whites. In eight short years, between 1710 and 1718, another forty-five hundred slaves were brought to Virginia. By the start of the American Revolution in 1776, the population of that state was evenly divided between whites and blacks.

Escaping Slavery

From the beginning of the slave trade, there were those who tried to escape. Some who were on slave ships jumped overboard, preferring suicide to life in bondage. Some groups aboard slave ships managed to overpower the crew. One of the most famous slave-ship revolts occurred in 1839 on the Spanish ship *Amistad* bound for Cuba. The revolt was led by Joseph Cinque, the son of an African king. Fifty-three slaves seized the *Amistad* and ordered the small crew to sail back to Africa. The sailors instead headed to the coast of North America, where the slaves were captured off the coast of Long Island.

Since slave importation was illegal in 1839, the Africans fought for their freedom in the courtrooms of the United States. John Quincy Adams, a former U.S. president, represented the slaves. The case went all the way to the Supreme Court, and the men were allowed to go free. This was one of the few

Slaves crowd the deck of a ship en route to the New World.

cases in which captured slaves were allowed to return to Africa.

Many other slaves continued to fight against their oppressors after they reached American shores. There were a few instances of widespread slave revolts, but most of these were put down and the slaves who planned them were killed. Other, more successful attempts to throw off the yoke of bondage involved individuals or small groups of slaves.

Some slaves were helped by Native Americans, who were also fighting against white settlers. They were taken in by tribes, and many lived their lives surviving in the American wilderness with the natives. In Florida, which was not part of the United States until 1819, the Seminole Indians were particularly friendly to escaped slaves, and some intermarried with Native Americans.

Other slaves were able to escape to the remote sea islands off the coast of South Carolina. The escaped slaves and their descendants established a culture called Geechee that continued to use African language and traditions long after they had disappeared elsewhere.

The journey was far more perilous for those who attempted to escape to the free states in the northern United States. Since it was illegal for slaves to attend school, most slaves could not read or follow a map. Some knew that if they followed the North Star, the brightest star in the Little Dipper constellation,

Runaway slaves could sometimes find safety with Native American tribes, who were also at odds with white settlers.

they would eventually reach the states in the North, where slavery was illegal.

The Journey North

Slavery was not always illegal in the North. The first slaves were Native Americans forced into servitude by the Puritans in Massachusetts. Even though the climate was cold and individual farms were too small to work with large numbers of field hands, slaves still worked, tending cattle and raising crops. In cities, slaves worked as carpenters, bakers, blacksmiths, and tailors.

But in the spirit of the Declaration of Independence and the American Revolution, Vermont and Pennsylvania freed their slaves through state constitutions in 1777. Massachusetts did the same in 1783. Other northern states soon followed these examples and abolished slavery through state constitutions, laws, or judicial decisions.

Around the same time that state governments were abolishing slavery, the first organized groups were formed to help fugitive slaves. In a letter written in 1786, George Washington, speaking of an escaped slave, complained that "a society of Quakers formed for such purposes, have attempted to liberate him." Later in the same year he wrote of one of his own slaves who had escaped: "The gentleman in whose care I sent him has promised every endeavor to apprehend him; but it is not easy to do this, when there are numbers who would rather facilitate the escape of slaves than apprehend them when they run away."[1]

In 1787, a Quaker teenager named Isaac T. Hopper organized a system for hiding fugitive slaves and aiding their escape. Within a few years, escaped slaves were offered help in a number of towns in New Jersey and Pennsylvania. Those who wanted slavery abolished were called abolitionists, and as the number of slaves in the South grew, so too did the number of people who helped them escape bondage.

Americans declared independence in 1776 and threw off the yoke of British rule in 1781. But even as white Americans were celebrating their new freedoms, slave owners were concerned about escaped slaves receiving help from abolitionists. The Revolutionary War had disrupted the economy in the South, and slaveholders were eager to get back to business. This meant that they needed a legal groundwork for retrieving their slaves who had fled to free states.

While members of the Constitutional Convention in Philadelphia were debating the exact wording of the U.S. Constitution, Article IV, Clause 2, known as the "fugitive slave and felon clause," read:

No person held to service or labor in one state under the laws thereof, escaping into another, shall, in consequence of any law or regulation therein, be discharged from such service or labor, but shall be delivered up on claim of the party to whom such service or labor may be due.[2]

Although the word *slave* was never used, the meaning of the clause is clear: Slaves who

Many slaves tried to escape their oppressors by fleeing to free states in the North.

The Long Road to Freedom   **11**

had fled to free states must be returned to their owners.

The law did little to deter those who were helping escaped slaves, and free states paid little attention to the clause. Slave states continued to push for a law to punish those who were helping runaways. In 1793 Congress passed the Fugitive Slave Act, which made it a crime to help an escaped slave or to prevent his or her arrest. Those who broke the law were subject to heavy fines and imprisonment. As with Article IV, Clause 2 in the Constitution, northern states ignored the Fugitive Slave Act. In fact, some states passed laws that forbid government officials from helping capture fugitives.

The Fugitive Slave Act did not stop the loss of slave "property" of southern planters, and their outcry on the subject forced the U.S. Congress to pass the Fugitive Slave Law in 1850. The provisions of this law stated that anyone interfering with the arrest or aiding the escape of a slave would be "subject to a fine not exceeding one thousand dollars, or imprison-ment not exceeding six months," and that person was liable for "civil damages to the party injured by such illegal conduct in the sum of one thousand dollars for each fugitive lost."[3]

Since the Fugitive Slave Act was generally ignored in free states, many free African Americans lived in northern states without worry. However, the Fugitive Slave Law of 1850 was more stringent and allowed slave hunters to travel north to capture runaways. Because the North was no longer a safe haven, many fugitive slaves sought freedom in Canada, where slavery was illegal.

A small number of slaves had been finding their way to Canada since the late eighteeth century. During the War of 1812, however, there were open hostilities between the United States and Canada, and many blacks fled to the enemy nation. According to nineteenth-century historian Wilbur H. Siebert,

Soldiers returning from the War to their homes in Kentucky and Virginia brought news of the disposition of the Canadian

Under the Fugitive Slave Act, owners had the right to reclaim runaway slaves.

An 1840 antislavery cartoon depicts northern states as dogs, forced to retrieve fugitive slaves that have fled to Canada.

government to defend the rights of the self-emancipated slaves under its jurisdiction. Rumors of this sort gave hope and courage to the blacks that heard it, and, doubtless, the welcome reports were spread by these among trusted companions and friends.[4]

By 1826 there were so many slaves living in Canada that slaveholders complained loudly to Henry Clay, the U.S. secretary of state. Clay asked the Canadian government to return the runaways to their owners, but Canada refused. The number of blacks escaping to Canada grew every year. By the late 1820s it became increasingly necessary for those individuals helping the runaways to work in an organized fashion to escape detection.

What is known today as the Underground Railroad did not come into existence until the early 1830s. Although it was neither underground nor a railroad, legend has it that the railroad got its name when a slave named Tice Davis escaped from the slave state of Kentucky to the free state of Ohio. Davis's owner, whose name is unknown, was in hot pursuit, but Davis somehow managed to escape. When the owner combed the countryside for Davis but could not find him, he concluded that Davis had escaped on an "underground road."

The Underground Railroad

As the rumor of the slave who escaped on the underground road spread, the story was embellished by those who told it. The first steam-powered locomotive called the *Tom Thumb* had made a successful run in 1830, and before long the story said that Davis had escaped on an underground *railroad*.

There never was anything as comfortable or as efficient as a railroad carrying slaves to freedom, because the journey had to be taken in strict secrecy, or "underground." But the term *underground railroad* caught on, and

An 1844 poster for the Underground Railroad advertises "seats free, irrespective of color."

soon other railroad terms were applied to the journey. These terms were easy for slaves to remember and therefore served to disguise the illegal activities of the railroad. Slaves were referred to as *parcels* or *passengers*, while those who hid them and helped them were called *conductors*. Homes that offered refuge were *depots* or *stations*, and the people who lived there were *stationmasters*.

Participation in the Underground Railroad was a secret activity or, as William Breyfogle says in *Make Free*, "a peculiarly American combination of the illegal, the idealistic, and the improvised. It had virtually no over-all organization, and needed no more than it had."[5]

Few written records of the activity on the Underground Railroad were kept, especially in the early days. No one knows the names of the countless slaves who escaped or the names of the people who helped them. But a few now-famous people who risked their lives and their freedom for the cause have left written records, and it is the stories of these people that have survived to this day from the era of American slavery.

1 A Slave's Life

By the mid–nineteenth century, slavery had existed in the United States for more than two hundred years. Over that time, slave traders had brought hundreds of thousands of slaves into the country. Slaves who had survived the torturous journey from Africa found new horrors upon arrival in North America. When a slave ship pulled into a port city's harbor, town criers strolled through the streets announcing the arrival of a fresh load of human cargo. Plantation owners stopped their farmwork and came down to the docks to purchase field hands and servants. Barefoot and half-naked men and women shivered in the unfamiliar cold climate as they were poked, prodded, and examined by prospective buyers. Within hours the slaves were sold at auction to the highest bidders. What lay ahead for most slaves was a lifetime of hard work and the lash of the whip.

Marriages and families meant little to the slave buyers. Husbands, wives, mothers, and children were separated and sold individually, and most never saw each other again. Indeed, families would be separated on purpose so that they could not coordinate an escape plan. Likewise, members of the same tribe were separated. Since Africans had more than one thousand languages, members of one tribe were generally not able to communicate with members of another tribe. This, too, served to quell the possibilities of rebellion.

By the time the United States passed a law prohibiting the importation of slaves from Africa, on January 1, 1808, nearly 1.5 million slaves lived in the southern states. And the buying and selling of American slaves continued in the South until the Civil War ended slavery in 1865.

A dealer inspects a slave before offering him for sale at a Virginia auction.

Treating People as Property

The corrupt institution of slavery forced southern states to pass a wide variety of laws that could somehow legally justify holding human beings as captives. Alabama had typical laws concerning slaves in the 1850s. On one hand, slaves were referred to as "property" of their masters, and the slave owed the master all of his or her time, labor, and services. Courts, police, and militia intervened against anyone who "tampered" with this control. On the other hand, slaves were acknowledged as people, and laws required masters to furnish them with adequate food, clothing, and shelter and to provide for them in sickness and in their old age. There are few records, however, of any slave master being arrested or taken to court for mistreatment of his slaves.

Slave masters struggled with this concept of people as property in different ways. Some were humane. Others demanded the utmost return on their investment.

Not all slave owners were white. In 1830 more than thirty-six hundred free blacks or persons of mixed ancestry owned slaves, and there were some blacks who owned plantations with up to one hundred slaves. Many more free blacks, however, located and purchased family members—husbands, wives, or children—and set them free.

Since slaves were almost exclusively African Americans, other sets of laws were necessary to define who, in the parlance of the day, was a Negro, and thus a slave, and who was not. The race of the mother determined the status of a child whose parents were of mixed races. The offspring of a black slave father and a white woman was free. The offspring of a white man and a black mother was a slave.

Because slaves were so valuable, women were encouraged to have many children. According to history professor and author Kenneth M. Stampp,

Many masters counted the [fertility] of Negro women as an economic asset and

Slave Clothing

Even with slave labor, some plantations struggled economically. For slaves on those plantations, rations of food and clothing were kept to bare minimums. In the autobiography *Narrative of the Life of Frederick Douglass: An American Slave*, Douglass describes the average clothing allowance for men, women, and children on the plantation where he lived.

"[A slave's] yearly clothing consisted of two coarse linen shirts, one pair of linen trousers, like the shirts, one jacket, one pair of trousers for winter, made of coarse negro cloth, one pair of stockings, and one pair of shoes; the whole of which could not have cost more than seven dollars. The allowance of the slave children was given to their mothers, or the old women having the

care of them. The children unable to work in the field had neither shoes, stockings, jackets, nor trousers, given to them; their clothing consisted of two coarse linen shirts per year. When these failed them, they went naked until the next allowance day. Children from seven to ten years old, of both sexes, almost naked, might be seen at all seasons of the year."

Douglass himself received nothing as a child. He was kept almost naked in summer and winter. On the coldest nights he would steal a bag used to carry corn to the mill and sleep in it on the cold, damp floor with his head in the bag and his feet sticking out. "My feet have been so cracked with frost, that the pen with which I am writing might be laid in the gashes."

This nineteenth-century illustration was created by abolitionists to show the cruelty and inhumanity of slavery.

encouraged them to bear children as rapidly as possible.... These masters knew that the resulting surpluses would be placed on the market....

For instance, a Virginia planter boasted ... [every] infant ... [was] worth two hundred dollars at current prices the moment it was born.[6]

Some slave women had consensual sexual relationships with their white masters; others were raped by their owners. The offspring of these unions could be kept or sold at the will of the master.

Although marriage between slaves was not formally recognized by law, on many plantations slaves did marry. If a slave married a person from another plantation, the two were not allowed to live together. Minnie Folkes, born a slave in Virginia, explained the marriage customs in her region:

As to marriage, when a slave wanted to marry, why he would jes' ask his master to go over an' ask de [other] master could he take un to himself dis certain gal fer a wife.... De master make dem both jump over a broom stick an' dey is pronounced man an' wife. Both stay wid same masters (I mean ef John marries Sally, John stay wid his ole master an' Sal' wid hers but dey had privilieges you know like married folks). Ef chillun was born all o' 'em no matter how many, 'longed to de master whar de woman stayed.[7]

Laws Governing Slaves

Laws prohibited slaves from having any rights that were guaranteed to whites under the U.S. Constitution. The legal code in Louisiana stated that "The master may sell [a slave], dispose of his person, his industry,

A mother is restrained as her child is torn from her arms to be sold to another owner.

and his labor; [a slave] can do nothing, possess nothing, nor acquire anything but what must belong to his master."[8]

Virtually the only way a white person could commit a crime with regard to a slave was to steal one. In Virginia, stealing a slave could result in a prison sentence from two to ten years. In Tennessee it was five to fifteen years, and in other states, slave theft could result in the death penalty. These laws were used against conductors on the Underground Railroad who helped spirit slaves to freedom.

Slaves were unable to obtain property by purchase or gift. They had no claim to civil rights and no freedom of movement, and they could not make contracts, including marriage contracts. Slaves who lived as married couples could separate at will or be sold separately by their masters. The children of slaves could be sold as well. Frederick Douglass, one of the most famous ex-slaves—and one of the most active supporters of the Underground Railroad—wrote about this practice in his 1845 book *Narrative of the Life of Frederick Douglass: An American Slave:*

My mother and I were separated when I was but an infant—before I knew her as my mother. It is a common custom, in the part of Maryland from which I ran away, to part children from their mothers at a very early age. Frequently, before the child has reached its twelfth month, its mother is taken from it, and hired out on some farm a considerable distance off, and the child is placed under the care of an old woman, too old for field labor. For what this separation is done, I do not know, unless it be to hinder the development of the child's affection toward its mother, and to blunt and destroy the natural affection of the mother for the child.[9]

Douglass went on to say that the bonds between himself and his mother remained. On four or five occasions, Douglass's mother walked twelve miles from her plantation to where her son lived. Even though this journey was exhausting, Douglass's mother had to return home the same night, for she risked a whipping if she was not in the fields at dawn.

Division of Plantation Labor

At its heart, slavery was an inhumane system of forced labor. Thousands of field hands were needed to clear the forests in order to build the system of plantations that existed in the southern United States. Thousands more were needed to plant, harvest, and process crops such as rice, indigo, tobacco, sugar, and cotton.

Large plantations were most likely to use slaves, but many farms in the South were small, and the families who lived on them might own only a few slaves. On these small farms of several hundred acres, it was not unusual to see a white man and his sons working beside the slaves in the fields. Masters who owned more than a half-dozen slaves were less likely to work the fields but still performed tasks such as repairing tools and oversaw the planting and harvesting.

Most slaves never saw their masters working in the fields, however, because the majority of slaves lived on large plantations where the owners acted as managers and businessmen of the agricultural enterprise. On these plantations, depending on size, there might be anywhere from twenty to five hundred slaves or more.

Large plantations required a greater specialization of labor. The field hands were divided into plow gangs and hoe gangs. Some slaves might work full-time at ditch digging, tending livestock, driving wagons, or cultivating family vegetable gardens. Henrietta Perry, an ex-slave born in Danville, Virginia, recalls her labor in tobacco (tobaccy) fields, written in 1936 in the dialect as she spoke it:

Tobaccy? Used to get sick of seein' de weed. Use to wuk fum sun to sun in dat

Large plantations owners depended on slave labor to turn a profit.

A Slave's Life **19**

old terbaccy field. Wuk till my back felt lak it ready to pop in two. Marse [master] ain' raise nothin' but terbaccy, ceptin' a little wheat an corn for eatin', an us black people had to look arter [after] dat 'baccy lak it was gold. . . . Git a lashin . . . effen you cut a leaf fo' it was ripe. Marse ain' cared what we do in de wheat an' corn fiel', cause dat warn't nothin' but food for us [slaves], but better not do nothin' to dem 'baccy leaves.[10]

In working the labor force, plantation owners employed one or more men as slave drivers. Sometimes the drivers worked the fields and set the pace of the field hands; other times they urged the gangs on with words or a whip. One South Carolina rice planter, quoted in Kenneth M. Stampp's *The Peculiar Institution*, outlined the duties of a slave driver:

Drivers are, under the Overseer, to maintain discipline and order on the place. They are to be responsible for the quiet of the negro-houses, for the proper performance of tasks, for the bringing out the people early in the morning, and for the immediate inspection of such things as the Overseer only generally superintends.[11]

Most plantations used female slaves, especially older women, to perform work such as cooking, caring for children, and nursing the sick. Old or partially disabled slaves might work spinning wool and cotton into yarn and weaving it into clothing. Others might be used as soap makers, candle makers, brewers, and bakers. Older men gardened, cared for the livestock, and cleaned the yard.

Domestic slaves who worked in the master's house, or "big house," might perform any number of tasks depending on the size of the plantation and wealth of the master. They served as coachmen, laundresses, seamstresses, cooks, footmen, butlers, housemaids,

A domestic slave fans guests at a plantation dinner party.

During the depths of the Great Depression in the 1930s, the U.S. government hired unemployed writers to record American history. In 1936, the all-Negro unit of the Virginia Writers' Project began interviewing ex-slaves who were still alive in Virginia. During the following year, the stories of more than three hundred elderly African Americans were written down. Although about half of those interviews were lost or destroyed, the rest are available in the book *Weevils in the Wheat*. (The title of the book refers to a term used by slaves to communicate that a secret meeting or dance had been discovered by the overseers and so canceled.)

In an effort to preserve the unique speech patterns of the ex-slaves, the stories were written down in the dialect spoken by the men and women interviewed. Thus the word *tobacco* might be spoken as "terbaccy" or "tobacca." *Master* might be written as "marse," and the word *they* as "dey." This technique of writing dialect was also used by other sources in this book. Since interviews were conducted by different people, words and spellings vary. Despite the often strange spellings, these interviews remain a valuable resource. As ex-slave Arthur Greene told an interviewer in *Weevils in the Wheat*,

"Lord, Lord, chile, what make you folks wait so long 'fo' you git dis stuff 'bout way bac' yonder? All us fellers 'most done gone to tother world. Well, God done spared a few o' us to tell de tale."

chambermaids, children's nannies, and personal servants.

There were also a substantial number of skilled slave artisans who might be trained as blacksmiths, carpenters, mechanics, brick and stone masons, furniture makers, wheelwrights, and so on. Lorenzo L. Ivy, born a slave in Virginia in 1850, recalls his father's skills as a shoemaker:

One day when [father] was loafin' 'round de house, he tuk a table fork an' made a little lass [last—a block shaped like a human foot used in making or repairing shoes]. . . . An den he tuk de lass an' made a little shoe. Old Judge Gilman [the master] saw him make an an' was very pleased. He put him at shoe makin'. Sent him all de way to Lynchburg to learn under a man named Fretwell. He studied hard an' became one of the bes' shoemakers in de state. After he learned, [Gilman] tuk him out an' hire him out to different shoe shops. Finally he let him hire himself out. Yessuh! Let him make his own bargains.[12]

Slavery in Towns and Cities

In addition to working on plantations, about 500,000 slaves worked in southern cities or towns. They cut wood for steamboats. In swamplands they cut juniper, oak, and cypress trees for shingles, barrels, fences, and rails. In North Carolina, slave gangs labored as lumberjacks. Thousands of slaves worked in the turpentine industry. Elsewhere slaves worked in sawmills, gristmills, fisheries, and stone quarries. According to Kenneth M. Stampp, "They mined gold in North Carolina, coal and salt in Virginia, iron in Kentucky and Tennessee, and lead in Missouri.

The grueling task of harvesting cotton generally began in the punishing heat and humidity of mid-August.

On river boats they were used as deck hands and firemen."[13] Slaves also built thousands of miles of roadbed, canals, and railroads throughout the South.

In southern cities and towns, slaves worked in almost every occupation. They monopolized the domestic services, and many Southerners in towns owned one or two slaves who were used to cook, keep house, and garden. City slaves worked in cotton mills, tanneries, shipyards, and bake houses and as dock workers and clerks in stores. Almost all of the thirteen thousand workers in Virginia's tobacco factories were slaves. Hotels, restaurants, and bars also used slave labor.

Masters who owned skilled slaves such as barbers, cabinetmakers, and shoemakers often set them up in shops and then collected the profits. When slaves performed tasks for people other than their masters, it was the masters who received monetary compensation for the use of their "property."

Agricultural work is governed by the seasons. The book *Negro Slavery in Louisiana* details the work schedule of the Comite Plantation near Clinton in 1857:

A general cleaning up followed the beginning of the new year. Rails were hauled and fences were repaired; stables were cleaned out and repaired if necessary. During a January cold snap twenty-five hogs were killed and salted down, and about a month later this pork was smoked. A new field was cleared, an operation which necessitated much rolling of logs and burning of brush. Slaves were constantly being sent on errands as the plantation readied itself for the real business of the year. Plowing began before the end of February. Small grains were planted in February or early March, and seed for the first corn crop was in the ground before the end of the third month. Usually the strongest men cut trees and plowed, while women and children burned brush and stalks from the previous year's crop, but there are records aplenty of women who wielded axes and wrestled with plows. On one plantation, at least, women rolled logs while men plowed, but this was not common. Plowing with the tools of the Old South was not an enviable task at best; breaking up a new ground demanded great strength and greater endurance.[14]

Women and children planted seeds in the ground after a plow had turned over the earth. Within weeks, the seedlings were up and it was time to hoe. For this task, every available hand was given a heavy hoe to chop grass and weeds growing up between the crop plants. Depending on the amount of rain, fields needed to be hoed several more times before the Fourth of July holiday, after which no further cultivation was necessary.

Cotton picking generally began in the punishing heat and humidity of mid-August. Cotton picking requires skill, and some workers were better at it than others. At harvest

Working Under the Lash

Although not all slaves were mistreated by their owners, those who were lived through a daily hell of relentless work, beatings, and whippings. Reverend W. P. Jacobs, born a slave in 1852, talks about the abuse suffered by his uncle Charlie, whose job it was to cut trees for fence rails. Jacobs was quoted in *Weevils in the Wheat*.

"After you cut down your tree, you'd top off the branches and wedge and split the tree to make [fence] rails. That was some job. Those who couldn't make the number [required] had a whipping coming when the [slave]-driver counted up that evening. Uncle Charlie was one of the slaves that couldn't get his number finished. Almost every night he would get 39 lashes and that made him sore as could be, and he wouldn't work well the next day.

[One day] the [slave]-driver . . . was beating Uncle Charlie pretty hard. Uncle Charlie made up his mind he wouldn't stand it any longer, so he jumped the . . . driver. They fought and Uncle Charlie won. Uncle Charlie ran away. He swam the Ohio and was almost drowned. That's where they caught him. They brought him back and scourged him mightily."

Some slave owners resorted to physical brutality to punish their slaves.

Uncle Charlie eventually met a conductor on the Underground Railroad who helped him escape to Chicago, where he became a Methodist minister.

time every able-bodied person was put to work bringing in the crops, including domestic workers, children, and skilled workers.

To harvest the fluffy white cotton, slaves spent their entire daylight hours in the fields, carrying sacks, moving down rows, and pulling the open cotton from the husks, or bolls. When the sack was full, it was emptied, weighed, and returned to the picker. Average slaves picked 150 to 200 pounds of cotton a day. Those who failed to reach the quota specified by the master were often whipped unmercifully.

Most plantations had a cotton gin on the premises, that mechanically separated the seeds from the cotton fluff. Gins, operated by manpower or horsepower, pressed the cotton lint into four-hundred-pound-bales. They were excessively slow, and gin crews often worked late into the night. Cotton gins were large, dangerous machines, and it was not unusual for a tired, underfed slave to lose a hand or arm in the spinning mechanisms of the gin.

After the crops were harvested, the rest of autumn was spent cleaning the gin house and the tools, processing and shipping the baled cotton, shucking and hauling corn and animal feed, cleaning and repairing irrigation ditches, cutting and hauling wood, and preparing new fields.

Slaves who cultivated rice, tobacco, hemp, or sugar worked a similar year-round routine, used the same basic tools, and performed many of the same tasks as those who worked in the cotton fields.

Working from Sunup to Sundown

The daily toil for field hands on a plantation began about an hour before sunrise. A man who worked on a Louisiana plantation describes a slave's life during harvest months:

An hour before daylight the horn is blown. Then the slaves arouse, prepare their breakfasts, fill a gourd with water, in another [gourd] deposit their dinner of

An owner weighs the day's cotton harvest as slaves look on.

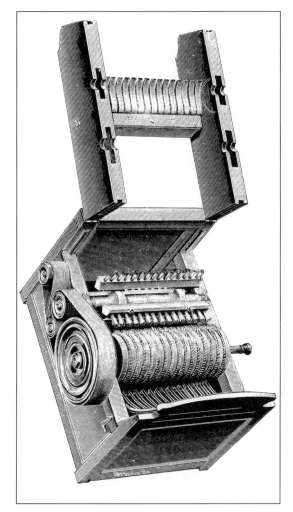

The cotton gin enabled efficient processing of hundreds of pounds of cotton a day.

With less daylight in winter, workdays were necessarily shorter. But on nights with a bright full moon, slaves might labor well past midnight. And there were few days in the year when a master could not find some essential work to keep his field hands busy. (It should be noted that at this time, white farmers, and even white northern factory workers, labored at least twelve hours a day, six days a week, for which they were paid very little.)

The treatment of slaves varied from plantation to plantation. Some masters were known for their kindness, many more known for their cruelties. In *Weevils in the Wheat*, Alice Marshall, born a slave in Virginia in 1850, recalls the evil nature of her marse (master) named Nuck Night:

> I kin recollect plenty things 'bout dem way back times. Dere was ole "Nuck" Night. Ev'ybody call him marse "Nuck." Didn't know his real name an' didn't keer much; he so mean to his slaves. . . . 'Tis hard to believe, but ole Marse ["Nuck"] kep' shackles on his niggers all the time. Kep' dey feet tied together wid chains so he could keep up wid 'em. He skeered dey run away. De onlyst time when he take off dem chains is when he wuk in de fiel'. An' he whipped his niggers unmercifully. Some time he whip 'em in de barn wid de bull whip; den agin he take 'em down de branch an' chain 'em to a tree where switches is everywhere. For every lick he give 'em dey say, "Pray Master." Some time we stan' in de corn fiel' listen' to de whippin's. All we hear is "Pow!" den, "Pray Master!" "Pow!" "Pray Master!" It went on lak dat sometime for hours. Den ole massa "Nuck" salt 'em down [with] braine [brine], so dey ain' miss nary day's wuk.[16]

cold bacon and corn cake, and hurry to the field again. It is an offense invariably followed by a flogging to be found at the quarters after daybreak. Then the fears and labors of another day begin; and until its close there is no such thing as rest. He fears he will be caught laggin through the day; he fears to approach the gin house with his basket of cotton at night; he fears, when he lies down, that he will oversleep himself in the morning.[15]

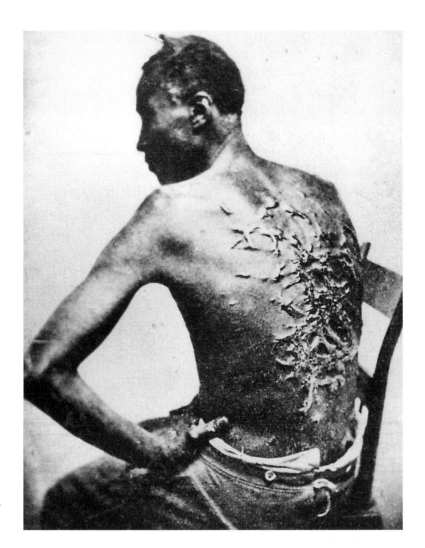

A cotton planter bears the scars of countless whippings by his master.

Slave Cabins

Most plantation workers lived with friends or members of their extended families in slave quarters, which were small cabins of log or board with mud plaster between the cracks. The cabins were usually some distance from the "big house" and were arranged in rows facing each other, which allowed easy inspection from slave drivers.

Some of the better cabins, which were usually about fifteen feet square, were furnished with stools, slabs for cooking, a shelf, and a pail. The cabin might be divided in two, with one side serving as a sleeping compartment where the floor was raised a foot or two above the ground. Pallets covered with moss or straw served as beds. Some slaves might have a chest of drawers in which their few personal belongings were kept. These types of cabins also had fireplaces where slaves could cook their meager meals, maybe roasting potatoes, cornmeal, or a piece of pork over hot coals.

Mrs. Georgia Gibbs, who was born a slave in 1849, recalls her childhood home:

Mastah give us huts to live in. De beds wuz made of long boards dat wuz nailed to de wall. De mattress wuz stuffed wif straw and pine tags. De only light we had wuz from de fire-place.[17]

Not all slaves lived in decent quarters. In *Plantation Slavery in Georgia*, Dr. John T. Turner mentions the slave cabins he observed in Georgia in 1857:

We have often seen them [slave huts] low, half-covered, half-ceiled and with half-made chimneys, where it is impossible for the inmates to dwell comfortable or warm at nights.[18]

In the same book, Dr. J. Dickonson Smith, who was concerned with the spread of epidemics, chided slave owners for poor quality housing:

"Small smoky cabins, built flat upon the ground, with no windows or aperture for ventilation, is the style that is too common." Dr. Smith added that he had treated many cases of typhoid fever among slaves due solely to these conditions.[19]

The Slave Diet

A typical slave diet consisted of cornmeal, bacon, and sometimes molasses. Seasonal vegetables and fruit might add to the monotonous diet. A staple of the diet was hoecake, which was "[corn]meal mixed with water in a thick batter. Got its name from some of 'em slappin' it on a hoe an' holdin' it in de fire place tell its cooked,"[20] according to Beverly Jones, an ex-slave born in 1848 in Court House, Virginia.

Those who were lucky enough to live on prosperous plantations were better fed. In

1937, Bailey Cunningham, a slave born in the 1830s in Starkey, Virginia, said his master was a rich man, and he recalled the food he ate as a child:

We ate twice a day, about sunup and at sundown. All the work hands ate in the cabins and all the children took their *cymblin* [squash] soup bowl to the big kitchen and got it full of cabbage soup, then we were allowed to go [to] the table where the white folks ate and get the crumbs from the table. We sat on the ground around the [slave] quarters to eat with wooden spoons. Rations were given to the field hands every Monday morning. They would go to the smokehouse and the misses would give us some meal and meat in our sack. We were allowed to go

While most plantation workers lived in small cabins like these, not all slaves received adequate living quarters.

A family eats hoe-cake, a dietary staple of slaves that consisted of cornmeal and water.

morning we would go to the smokehouse and get some flour and a piece of meat with a bone so we could have a hoe-cake for dinner on Sunday. Sometimes we had plenty of milk and coffee.[21]

Many other slaves were fed much less. Some suffered the torments of their masters when they were driven by hunger to steal food. Former slave William Brooks recalled his meager rations:

> Dey use to gib de slaves bout 6 pounds meat an' 5 pounds o' flour a week effen you ain' got chillun. If you got chillun, you git a little mo'. Well dat ain' 'nough lasten a dog a day. So dem [slaves] steal an' cose when dey steal dey git caught, an' when you git caught you git beat. I seen 'em take 'em in-a-de barn an' jes' tie 'em over lak dis an' den beat 'em so bad day run an' hide in de woods.[22]

The lack of food, the cruel treatment, and the dirty, smoky cabins were destructive to the health and well-being of slaves who were forced to endure such deprivations. Such conditions also strangled the spirits and souls of the slaves. It was for these reasons—and many others—that a constant stream of slaves chose to leave their families and their familiar surroundings to venture into the wilderness, running north into the unknown for a taste of freedom.

to the garden or field and get cabbage, potatoes and corn or any other vegetables and cook in our shanties. We had plenty to eat. We had a large iron baker with a lid to bake bread and potatoes and a large iron kettle to boil things in. On Saturday

2 Life on the Run

As the nineteenth century progressed, protests against slavery from both black and white people grew louder and more insistent. Plantation owners attempted to justify their use of slaves by claiming that their "bondsmen" were content with their servitude and that most were treated with kindness—and since most slaves by that time were born into bondage, they knew of no other life. This attitude was the main argument against ending slavery, an argument that was belied by the constant quest for freedom exercised by runaway slaves.

Those held in captivity needed only to look at their masters and other free people to see the advantages of freedom. Even in the Deep South there was a small minority of blacks who had been granted freedom by their masters or had worked after hours at extra jobs in order to buy their way out of slavery. These freedmen, as they were called, were considered by slaveholders to be a bad influence on slaves. Many whites wanted to expel all free black persons from the South. One group in Charleston, South Carolina, wrote to a judge:

> [Slaves] continually have before their eyes, persons of the same color, many of whom they have known in slavery . . . freed from the control of their masters, working where they please, going whither they please, and expending their money how they please.[23]

There is little doubt that the great majority of those in bondage wished to enjoy these benefits offered by freedom.

Longing in their Hearts for Freedom

Many people assumed that slaves who lived under the harshest conditions were the people most likely to escape. But former slave Frederick Douglass had a different opinion:

> Beat and cuff your slave, keep him hungry and spiritless, and he will follow the chain of his master, like a dog; but feed and clothe him well,—work him moderately—surround him with physical comfort,—and dreams of freedom intrude. Give him a *bad* master, and he aspires to a *good* master; give him a good master, and he wishes to become his *own* master. Such is human nature. You may hurl a man so low, beneath the level of his kind, that he loses all just ideas of his natural position; but elevate him a little, and the clear conception of rights rises to life and power, and leads him onward.[24]

Perhaps the natural human longing for freedom was best expressed by an unnamed white man who once testified before the Louisiana Supreme Court with these words: The desire for freedom "exists in the bosom of *every* slave—whether the recent captive, or him to whom bondage has become a habit."[25]

Frederick Douglass

Frederick Douglass was born a slave in Maryland in 1817 and became one of the most famous African American abolitionists—as well as one of the greatest American public speakers—of his time. Douglass was taught the alphabet at a young age by his master's wife and later taught himself to read and write.

In 1838 Douglass escaped to New Bedford, Massachusetts, where he came into contact with the Massachusetts Anti-Slavery Society. By 1841, the society enlisted Douglass as a public speaker because of his skillful oratory.

In speech after speech, Douglass told of the horrors of slavery and called for its immediate abolition. His speaking manner was so smooth, however, that people began to doubt that he had actually ever been a slave. To dispel this distrust, in 1845 Douglass published his autobiography entitled *Narrative of the Life of Frederick Douglass*, which was later renamed *Life and Times of Frederick Douglass*.

Douglass later traveled to the British Isles, where he became something of a celebrity because of his antislavery speeches. Upon returning to the United States, he settled in Rochester, New York, where he founded his newspaper, the *North Star* (later renamed *Frederick Douglass' Paper*). While living in Rochester, Douglass often offered his home as an Underground Railroad station to fugitive slaves on their way to Canada.

When the Civil War broke out, Douglass convinced the government to allow black men in the Union army and recruited the 54th and 55th Massachusetts Colored Regiments, which later won distinction in battle. After the war Douglass served on several federal government committees and was U.S. minister to Haiti from 1889 to 1891. A true reformer to the end, Douglass died on February 20, 1895, when he collapsed after attending a meeting organized to obtain voting rights for women.

Former slave Frederick Douglass was an important leader of the abolitionist movement.

A look at a map showing free states and slave states shows just how far slaves needed to travel to find freedom. Slave states covered a huge area of the continental United States, from Alabama, Mississippi, and Louisiana on the Gulf of Mexico all the way up to Kentucky, West Virginia, Tennessee, the Carolinas, Virginia, and Maryland. Only a narrow band of states provided relative safety for runaways, including Ohio, Indiana, Illinois, Iowa, Pennsylvania, and New York.

Most of those who escaped came from northern regions of the South such as Kentucky and Maryland, where fugitives had a relatively short distance of one hundred miles to travel. Those in the Deep South states of Alabama, Mississippi, and Louisiana had much slimmer chances of evading their captors through six hundred or seven hundred miles of hostile territory. For those who lived in the Deep South, liberty beckoned from other directions: Some slaves escaped to the Bahamas; Arkansas slaves fled west to Native American territory; and Texas runaways fled to Mexico. Sometimes bands of runaways fled into the deep forests or swamps, where they established camps and built huts in which to live. Some grew their own food; others obtained it by raiding nearby farms. In one such camp in South Carolina, fugitives lived in a

clearing surrounded by a dense thicket and killed hogs and sheep they took from local farmers. For most slaves, however, the route north to Canada on the Underground Railroad was the main road to freedom.

There is no accurate record of how many slaves ran away; how many were caught, returned, and punished; and how many succeeded in finding freedom. There were, however, hundreds of notices in local newspapers offering rewards for returned slaves and some records kept by conductors and stationmasters on the Underground Railroad. A reasonable estimate came in 1855 by a judge who claimed that, by that time, the South had lost up to sixty thousand slaves.

Many escaped slaves bore the whip marks of a cruel master on their bodies. Runaways were usually young men under the age of thirty, but female fugitives and older slaves were by no means uncommon. Skilled artisans ran away, as did field hands. Some ran

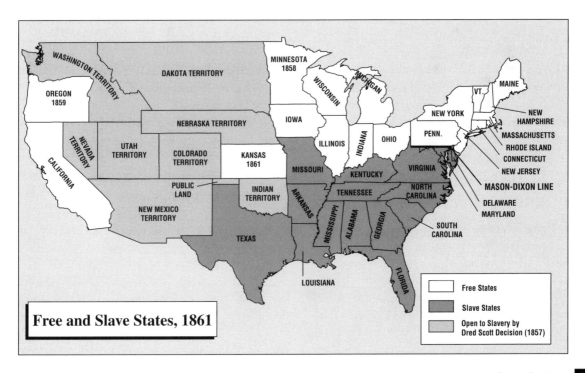

Free and Slave States, 1861

Free States

Slave States

Open to Slavery by Dred Scott Decision (1857)

RUNAWAYS.

TWENTY-FIVE DOLLARS RE- WARD. — Runaway from my place, in Chesterfield county, Va., my Negro Man BEN JOHNSON, of black color, about 5 feet 10 inches high, weighs about 175 lbs., apparently 45 or 50 years old, and is a good cook, and is probably hiring himself to cook in Richmond or Petersburg. The above reward will be paid for his safe delivery to me at PULLIAM & Co.'s office, or safe lodgment in some jail. He came from Petersburg. Left home 1st March last.
ap 17—tf   ALBERT C. PULLIAM.

$25 REWARD.—Runaway, on the 29th of March, a woman named NANCY, whom I purchased of H. Stern, of this city. She is of medium size, rather spare made, of a ginger-bread color, has a diffident look when spoken to, is twenty-three years old, has a blister scar on her neck. She was sold last Christmas at the sale of Wm. Andrews, dec'd, nine miles above the city. She may now be in that neighborhood, or near Slash Cottage, as she has a mother living at Mr. Wm Winn's, near that place, in Hanover county. She was hired to Mr. Samuel Allen, of this city, last year, and has a husband hired to Mr. Ballard, at the Exchange Hotel, by the name of Dolphius. I will pay the above reward if delivered to me in Richmond.
ap 16—1w*   R. B. WOODWARD.

An announcement offers rewards for the capture and return of fugitive slaves.

away frequently, others only once. Slaves usually went alone or in small groups, but there were cases of up to fifty slaves escaping at one time. Most ran off in the warm summer months when sleeping outdoors was possible. Others fought winter cold, wind, rain, and snow in pursuit of their freedom.

Escaping from Slavery

No fugitive slaves could reach the helpful arms of the conductors and stationmasters on the Underground Railroad without first taking flight from their plantations and making their way to the North through hostile territory. The prospect of capture and the fear of

the unknown made the hopes of a successful escape very discouraging. Frederick Douglass described the anxieties he and several other slaves felt when they planned to run away. They wondered if the owner would discover their plot and if he could read their thoughts through their behavior. Douglass said he often wondered whether bondage would be easier than the doubts, fears, and uncertainties. When planning their escape, Douglass imagined that

At every gate through which we had to pass, we saw a watchman; at every ferry, a guard; on every bridge, a sentinel; and in every wood, a patrol or slave-hunter. We were hemmed in on every side. . . . Upon either side, we saw grim death assuming a variety of horrid shapes. Now, it was starvation, causing us, in a strange and friendless land, to eat our own flesh. . . . Now, we were hunted by dogs, and overtaken and torn to pieces by their merciless fangs. We were stung by scorpions—chased by wild beasts—bitten by snakes. . . . No man can tell that intense agony which is felt by the slave, when wavering on the point of making an escape.[26]

Once slaves made the break, their methods of escape were as diverse as the escapees. In the early days, most of the fugitives were men who traveled on foot at night, usually through the woods to avoid detection. In later years, passengers included women and chil-

Slaves who escaped from the southern states often crossed hundreds of miles of hostile territory on foot.

dren, who might be transported by free blacks in wagons fitted with false bottoms or secret compartments that were covered with hay or other cargo. Most escapes involved several means of transportation, including horseback, covered wagons, large and small boats, carriages, and even trains, with fugitives hiding in box cars or posing as free blacks using train tickets supplied by conductors on the Underground Railroad.

Escape was difficult for many reasons. After leaving behind friends, family, and at least some guarantee of food, fugitives often wandered aimlessly for days. They had no maps and only the North Star to guide them. On cloudy nights, escapees felt trees with their hands, knowing that moss grew longest on the north sides of the bark. Since they could carry very little, some fugitives who owned clothing wore all of it in layers. Others suffered in the cold, sometimes losing fingers, toes, and ears to frostbite.

Outsmarting the Slave Hunters

Runaways could not stop and ask directions. Knowledge of the surrounding territory came by word of mouth. Well-known landmarks such as lakes, rivers, or rocky outcroppings were a much welcomed sight to fugitives. To throw off the hounds that were certain to pursue them, some learned to rub their shoes (if they had any) with red onion or spruce pine.

A slave named Mingo White tells how his friend Ned outsmarted the police (known as patrollers) and used them to find the proper route North:

Ned . . . tol' me de night he left the patterollers come in de woods lookin' for him, so he jes' got [in] a tree . . . an' den followed [after they passed]. Dey figured

[Ned] was headin' for de free states, so dey headed dat way too, and Ned jes' followed dem far as dey could go. Den he climb a tree an hid whilst dey turn 'roun' an' come back. Ned went on wid' out any trouble much.[27]

Runaway slaves faced the constant danger of being pursued by slave hunters.

Some fugitives managed to arm themselves with guns and knives and were able to hunt. But many had to walk hundreds of miles—up to twenty miles a day—with little or no food except the occasional wild berries or food stolen from farmyards. Some slaves were helped by southern members of the Underground Railroad. Others were offered help by someone who soon betrayed them in order to collect a reward. Common routes north were often guarded by dangerous gangs of slave hunters who collected bounties for the fugitives they returned. Oftentimes the fearful enterprise ended in the tragedy of failure and certain punishment.

Once fugitive slaves managed to reach the free states, however, there were many more people working for the Underground Railroad. And their established methods helped aid those on their way to Canada. Runaways were taught codes they could use as they traveled from farm to farm such as secret knocks and passwords that stationmasters would recognize. Since many stationmasters

Advertising Rewards for Runaways

One of the main sources of ad revenue for nineteenth-century southern newspapers were the countless ads slave masters ran offering rewards for their runaway slaves. *The Underground Rail Road*, written by African American author William Still in 1871, has several examples of these ads.

"William N. Taylor
ONE HUNDRED DOLLARS REWARD.
—Ran away from Richmond City on Tuesday, the 2d of June, a negro man named Wm. N. TAYLOR, belonging to Mrs. Margaret Tyler of Hanover county.

Said negro was hired to Fitzhugh Mayo, Tobacconist; is quite black, of genteel and easy manners, about five feet ten or eleven inches high, has one front tooth broken, and is about 35 years old.

He is supposed either to have made his escape North, or attempted to do so. The above reward will be paid for his delivery to Messrs. Hill and Rawlings, in Richmond, or secured in jail, so that I can get him again.
JAS. G. TYLER,
Trustee for Margaret Tyler.
Richmond Enquirer, June 9, 57."

were Quakers, mentioning the name of American Quaker leader William Penn opened doors. Some fugitives obtained forged papers that showed them to be a free black person, but this ruse was easily detected under the intense scrutiny of the slave hunters, and it was used only as a last resort.

Stories of Freedom and Horror

Abolitionist newspapers were filled with hundreds of stories that detailed the hardships endured by slaves who were in pursuit of freedom. The tales range from the ingenious to the horrifying. Slaves who lived near the seacoast or along major rivers were sometimes able to convince steamship captains—many of whom were Northerners—to allow them to hide aboard their ships. Other times black deckhands helped hide the fugitives beneath the decks.

Despite the $1,000 reward offered for her, Clarissa Davis escaped detection and reached Underground Railroad conductors by dressing as a man and stowing away in a box on a steamship in Portsmouth, Virginia. According to William Still's 1872 book *The Underground Rail Road*, another runaway, James Mercer, was also delivered to a northern Underground Railroad station by steamship, but Mercer had to hide

> not far from the boiler, where the heat and coal dust were almost intolerable. . . . Nor was he certain that [he] could endure the intense heat of that place. It admitted of no other posture than lying flat down, wholly shut out from the light, and nearly in the same predicament in regard to the air. Here, however, was a chance of throwing off the yoke, even if it cost [him his] life.[28]

THE

UNDERGROUND RAIL ROAD.

A RECORD

OF

FACTS, AUTHENTIC NARRATIVES, LETTERS, &C.,

Narrating the Hardships Hair-breadth Escapes and Death Struggles

OF THE

Slaves in their efforts for Freedom,

AS RELATED

BY THEMSELVES AND OTHERS, OR WITNESSED BY THE AUTHOR;

TOGETHER WITH

SKETCHES OF SOME OF THE LARGEST STOCKHOLDERS, AND
MOST LIBERAL AIDERS AND ADVISERS,
OF THE ROAD.

BY

WILLIAM STILL,

For many years connected with the Anti-Slavery Office in Philadelphia, and Chairman
of the Acting Vigilant Committee of the Philadelphia Branch of
the Underground Rail Road.

Illustrated with 70 fine Engravings by Bensell, Schell and others, and
Portraits from Photographs from Life.

Thou shalt not deliver unto his master the servant that has escaped from his master unto thee.—*Deut.* xxiii. 15.

SOLD ONLY BY SUBSCRIPTION.

PHILADELPHIA:
PORTER & COATES,
822, CHESTNUT STREET.
1872.

An advertisement for William Still's 1872 book offers narratives of "hardships, hair-breadth escapes and death struggles" along the Underground Railroad.

Steamships were not the only public transportation used to reach Underground Railroad stations. A slave known only as John made his way north from Alabama atop a railroad car. John climbed aboard at night and when the train stopped around daylight, he slipped off the top of the car and hid in the woods until dark. The next night he climbed on top of another railcar. By this method he reached an Underground Railroad station in Virginia.

Not all slaves ran away using such traditional methods. Henry Box Brown earned his middle name by escaping inside a mailing crate.

Life on the Run

Suddenly, as if from above, there darted into my mind these words, "Go and get a box, and put yourself in it.". . . I then repaired to a carpenter, and induced him to make me a box [two feet eight inches deep, two feet wide, and three feet long].

When the box was finished, I carried it, and placed it before my friend, who had promised to assist me. . . . I took my place in this narrow prison, with a mind full of uncertainty as to the result. . . . I laid me down in my darkened home of three feet by two, and like one about to be guillotined, resigned myself to my fate. . . .

I took with me a bladder to be filled with water to bathe my neck with, in case of too great heat; and with no access to the fresh air, excepting three small [drill] holes, I started my perilous cruise. . . . I was first carried to the express office, the box being placed on its end, so that I started with my head downwards. . . . I was put aboard a steamboat *and placed on my head*. In this dreadful position, I remained . . . when I began to feel of my eyes and head, and found to my dismay, that my eyes were almost swollen out of their sockets, and the veins on my temple seemed ready to burst.[29]

Brown's box was eventually turned over, and he survived his journey to Philadelphia, where he was happily received by stationmasters on the Underground Railroad.

Other fugitive slaves, such as Levi Douglass, used personal skills and intelligence to escape from their captors. Levi ran away from his master, but he was chased down and captured by a party of twenty-five men. His story was printed in the *Anti-Slavery Reporter* in March 1853.

Levi was taken and put in [jail], where he was duly advertised as a runaway. There he was confined five weeks, waiting the arrival of his owner. In the meantime, being an excellent dancer, he managed to get into the good graces of his [jailer], who invited white people to come and see his feats. They often gave him pieces of money, and, finding that his keeper was fond of whisky, [Levi] liberally supplied [the jailer] with it out of the proceeds. Having made arrangements for his escape from this prison-house, he seized his opportunity, when his keeper was in a state of complete intoxication. . . . [Levi] fled a second time for Ohio, where, after incredible fatigue, and almost famished from want of food, he safely arrived. There he fell in with the managers of the "Underground Railroad," and was soon placed by them in a position of comparative safety. After labouring some time in the country, he removed to Cleveland, and there he became a waiter in one of the hotels.[30]

Levi eventually bought a plot of farmland in Canada. His happy story, however, is tempered by the fact that his mother and eight of his brothers and sisters remained in the hands of four different slaveholders in Virginia.

Crossing into Free Territory

The Ohio River between Kentucky and the free state of Ohio is swift flowing, deep, and wide—and a major obstruction for fugitives on the road to freedom. With only a few suitable crossing points, it was easy for slave hunters to watch the river and search for their prey. Edward Walker, a slave in Kentucky, describes his journey across the river and his escape to Canada:

Most fugitives traveled at night to avoid capture by slave hunters.

Early in 1858 my brother and I worked out a plan of escape. My brother was married to a girl that lived on a plantation four miles away and they had a little daughter. A colored man, who was also a slave, helped us. . . . He fixed matters with a white agent of the underground railroad in Cincinnati, who agreed to have a boat waiting for us on the river bank . . . in Covington [Kentucky]. On a Wednesday night we started out to escape. . . .

We had to be very cautious for a guard was supposed to be watching for runaways every night on the river bank. We had to cross a piece of quicksand about twelve feet across before we got to the bank. I didn't know what it was so I stood on it and handed my brother's wife and child across. Then my brother passed over. . . . I turned to go, too, when I found that I was stuck. I could not pull my feet out and I felt I was sinking. I didn't dare to call out as I was afraid the guard would catch us.

It was rather hard work, but [my brother] pulled me out. We all got in the small boat and the white agent rowed us across to Cincinnati. We were taken to the house of a colored family and stayed there about a week and then left for Canada. My brother and his family and myself rode in one buggy with a white driver. The other buggy was occupied by three fugitives—one woman and two men—and a white man as driver. We travelled at night and slept in farmers' houses by day.[31]

Like Ohio, Indiana was a free state that bordered Kentucky, and many white farmers there acted as stationmasters and were glad to help African Americans escape. A Kentucky slave named Daly describes his journey on the Underground Railroad through Indiana and into Canada:

I made arrangements to run away myself, with my children . . . all my children could ride except the youngest one, who was two years old. . . . They went to the river bank in front of the farm [where I lived], and there I came with my daughter Mary. I had a boat all ready and rowed it across to Indiana. Everything was ready. We mounted horses and I took my youngest girl in my arms. We rode very fast every night. One party of underground railway agents would ride with us along the road until midnight, when another party would ride with us until nearly daylight. We stopped at farm houses in the day time. Then we took the Michigan Central [train] cars at a station,

Life on the Run

I don't remember the name, and we came into Detroit.[32]

Although 60,000 to 100,000 slaves managed to reach freedom, Canada was a foreign land to African Americans where—although slavery was illegal—prejudice against blacks was common. In addition, the joy of liberty was often tempered by the pain of being separated from loved ones who were often left behind in slavery. A letter from Samuel W. Johnson, who had escaped to Canada, to his wife, who remained a slave, demonstrates that pain:

My dearest wife I have Left you and now I am in a foreign land about fourteen hundred miles from you but . . . my thoughts are upon you all the time . . . my mind [is] with you night and day the Love that I bear for you in my breast is greater than I thought it was. . . . I am destitute of money I have not got in no business yet but when I do get into business I shall write you and also remember you. Tell my Mother and Brother and all enquiring friends that I am now safe in a free state and cant tell where I am at present.[33]

Johnson's letters were mailed to a conductor on the Underground Railroad to be smuggled to his wife's plantation. It is doubtful they ever reached her.

Lives of the Trackers

The Fugitive Slave Act of 1793 gave any white man the authority to arrest a runaway slave. After the arrest, the slave was brought before a judge of the circuit or district court of the United States or before a local magistrate where the capture was made. After displaying proof of ownership such as purchase receipts or plantation records, warrants were issued to allow the slave hunter to return the prisoner back to the state from which he or she had fled.

Since any white man could capture runaways, many—tempted by rewards—made a profession of it. Poor white men with the hope of financial windfalls, made it a habit to watch the roads for people who looked like fugitives. Any African American, whether free or slave, who was caught without proper papers, was subject to violent capture. And most poor whites had little sympathy for the problems faced by black slaves, as shown in this article in the July 1, 1850, *Baltimore Sun:*

> White workingmen on the Baltimore and Susquehanna Railroad caught several Maryland bondsmen who had escaped to within five miles of the Pennsylvania border. The workingmen returned them to their owners and collected the reward.[34]

Slave Patrols

A slave was legally considered a runaway if he or she was caught a certain distance from home. In Mississippi that distance was eight miles; in Missouri it was twenty. These laws were generally enforced by police organizations known as

Eager to collect reward money, slave hunters shoot down escaped slaves.

Slave hunters frequently used bloodhounds to track down runaway slaves.

slave patrols. Every slave state had these patrols, which were loosely affiliated with the state militias. In Virginia each county employed an officer and at least four militiamen who were paid with an exemption from taxes. According to *A History of Slavery in Virginia*, the patrollers were authorized to

> arrest all such persons or strolling slaves and servants without passes, and to take them to a justice to be whipped not exceeding twenty lashes. . . . A special patrol, a captain, and three men, were provided for . . . to recapture fugitive slaves. It was paid a reasonable compensation from the fugitive slave tax and the master was also assessed, according to distance, from $40 to $100 for the captive. . . . When the slaves escaped to a great distance special methods and rewards had to be provided for their recovery, and these in the absence of a national fugitive slave law were not often successful. A reward of 15 per cent. of the value of the slave was offered for those returned from Allegheny, Washington, and Frederick counties, Maryland, and 25 per cent. of his value if returned from a free State. For the nearer counties on the Ohio and

Potomac 10 per cent. only was offered. For slaves captured in Ohio, Pennsylvania or Indiana a reward of 50 per cent. and mileage 20 cents a mile, and if in New England, New York or Canada $120.[35]

If the master lived far away or could not be located, the fugitive was delivered to jail, where he or she would stay from three months to a year. All the while, notices would be run in newspapers announcing that the slave had been caught. If the slave owner still did not come forward, the slave could be auctioned off to the highest bidder. The proceeds of the sale would be given to the master if he should ever come forward—minus rewards, jail fees, and other costs.

Hunting Fugitive Slaves

Dogs, particularly bloodhounds, were almost always employed to hunt fugitive slaves. The practice, deplored by abolitionists, was defended and justified throughout the South. Gangs of slave owners sometimes rode through fields and swamps with packs of dogs searching for runaways in a sport compared to fox hunting. Professional slave hunters often advertised that they had packs of "Negro dogs" trained to hunt fugitives. Others specialized in training and selling "Negro dogs."

Dogs could follow a scent twenty-four hours after a runaway had traveled through an area. Once the slave was caught, slave hunters often allowed the dogs to bite their hunted prey. Many slaves were pulled from trees by dogs and were severely mauled. Hunters shrugged off such brutality, thinking it would "cure" the fugitive from further escape.

Southern slave codes required any officers of the law to assist in the recapture of slaves. The same codes required that the owner of a fugitive pay the slave hunter for his troubles. Kentucky obligated the slave holder to pay $100 for runaways taken in states where slavery was illegal. In Texas slaves escaped to Mexico, and Mexican slave hunters were promised a reward equal to one-third of a slave's value to return the fugitives across the border.

Professional Kidnappers

The Fugitive Slave Law of 1850 enabled a master or his agent to claim a slave even in a free state. Fugitives in the North had to be wary of professional slave catchers. One such man, F. H. Pettis, a New York City lawyer, placed advertisements in southern newspapers claiming that he was an experienced slave hunter. Masters who wanted to employ the services of Pettis were asked to forward a description of the slave and $20. If the runaway was captured, an extra $100 charge was to be paid.

The lure of the reward was so strong that, on occasion, white men who encountered slaves on errands in town would urge slaves to

Illegal Words

To maintain their way of life, slave owners made sure that state legislatures passed strict laws against helping runaway slaves. Despite the First Amendment of the U.S. Constitution, which guarantees free speech, it was made illegal to write or say anything that might inspire a slave to escape. *The Peculiar Institution* by Kenneth M. Stampp details some state laws from the days of slavery.

"The codes were quite unmerciful toward whites who interfered with slave discipline. Heavy fines were levied upon persons who . . . taught [slaves] to read or write. North Carolina made death the penalty for concealing a slave 'with the intent and for the purpose of enabling such slave to escape.' Every slave state made it a felony to say or write anything that might lead, directly or indirectly, to discontent or rebellion; in 1837, the Missouri legislature passed an act 'to prohibit the publication, circulation, and promulgation of the abolition doctrines.' The Virginia code of 1849 provided a fine and imprisonment for any person who maintained 'that owners have no right of property in their slaves.' Louisiana made it a capital offense to use 'language in any public discourse, from the bar, the bench, the stage, the pulpit, or in any place whatsoever' that might produce 'insubordination among the slaves.' Most southern states used their police power to prohibit the circulation of 'incendiary' material through the United States mail; on numerous occasions local postmasters, public officials, or mobs seized and destroyed antislavery publications."

run away, then catch them to collect the bounty. Other times, free blacks would betray runaway slaves for the same money-driven motive.

People used many different tricks to fool even the most careful fugitive into self-incrimination. One story was related in *Make Free* by William Breyfogle:

> A runaway named Henry . . . let himself be duped by people of his own race. Henry had escaped to Pennsylvania, but was uneasy about being retaken. He was advised to consult a Negro fortune-teller. The fortune-teller asked his name when

A post-bill warns slaves to be on the lookout for professional kidnappers.

CAUTION!!
COLORED PEOPLE
OF BOSTON, ONE & ALL,
You are hereby respectfully CAUTIONED and advised, to avoid conversing with the
Watchmen and Police Officers of Boston,
For since the recent ORDER OF THE MAYOR & ALDERMEN, they are empowered to act as
KIDNAPPERS
AND
Slave Catchers,
And they have already been actually employed in KIDNAPPING, CATCHING, AND KEEPING SLAVES. Therefore, if you value your LIBERTY, and the *Welfare of the Fugitives* among you, *Shun* them in every possible manner, as so many *HOUNDS* on the track of the most unfortunate of your race.
Keep a Sharp Look Out for KIDNAPPERS, and have TOP EYE open.
APRIL 24, 1851.

he was a slave, his master's name, and where he had come from. With this information, and for a consideration of ten dollars, the fortune-teller promised to cast a spell that would protect against recognition or recapture by his former owner. Henry gave all the information asked and paid the fee. The fortune-teller then wrote to the master, and no doubt pocketed a reward. Henry was easily captured, and was later sold in Natchez for the high price of $1,800.[36]

This atmosphere of mistrust weighed heavily on any slave who managed to escape to a free state. Frederick Douglass eloquently described his fears after successfully reaching New York after running from a plantation in Maryland:

> I was afraid to speak to anyone for fear of speaking to the wrong one, and thereby falling into the hands of money-loving kidnappers, whose business it was to lie in wait for the panting fugitive, as the ferocious beasts of the forest lie in wait for their prey. The motto which I adopted —when I started from slavery was this— "trust no man!" I saw in every white man an enemy, and in almost every colored man cause for distrust. It was a most painful situation; and, to understand it, one must needs experience it, or imagine himself in similar circumstances. Let him be a fugitive slave in a strange land—a land given up to be hunting-ground for slave holders—whose inhabitants are legalized kidnappers—where he is every moment subjected to the terrible liability of being seized upon by his fellow-men, as the hideous crocodile seizes upon his prey!—I say, let him place himself in my situation . . . and . . . let him feel that he is

Living and working among millions of African American slaves in the South were thousands of free blacks who managed to evade the shackles of slavery. Some free blacks were emancipated by their former masters; several managed to buy their freedom; others were born free.

These blacks were looked on with fear and hatred by southern whites because they were living proof that blacks could successfully function as free men and women. The very presence of free blacks was thought to cause unhappiness in slaves, who might be enticed to escape in order to emulate the independence of the free men and women.

Slave hunters and patrollers were often just as harsh to free blacks as they were to slaves. Any free black caught without papers might be quickly sold into slavery. Slave codes also dealt harshly with free blacks. Free blacks could not move from one state to another, and those who left their own state could not return. In South Carolina, free black sailors were rounded up by patrollers and forced to live in jail while their vessels were in port. Many Southerners called for free blacks to be driven from the South and for the reenslavement of those who would not leave.

A nineteenth-century illustration depicts a white couple commenting "poor things!" as they pass by freed blacks. Some whites believed blacks would not be capable of living without the support of their masters.

pursued by merciless men-hunters, and in total darkness as to what to do, where to go, or where to stay,—perfectly helpless both as to the means of defense and means of escape . . . among fellow-men, yet feeling as if in the midst of wild beasts, whose greediness to swallow up the trembling and half-famished fugitive is only equalled by that with which the monsters of the deep swallow up the helpless fish upon which they subsist.[37]

The Professional Slave Hunters

To some, slave hunting was simply a business. These individuals worked as speculators and bought the property rights to a slave who had escaped from an owner. The speculator paid a small percentage of the slave's worth with the hope of catching the fugitive and reselling him or her at a profit. This, in the jargon of the trade, was known as "buying them running." The story of two Maryland slave

Many fugitive slaves risked their lives fighting off slave hunters, rather than return to a life of slavery.

hunters, Joseph Ennells and Captain Frazer, is an example of these types of slave hunters at work.

In 1802, according to William Breyfogle, Frazer and Ennells "bought slaves running" and went to Philadelphia to search for the fugitives who were now legally their property. On their way, they arrested a free black man named William Bachelor, who was sixty years old. When another slave, who Ennells and Frazer brought from Maryland, testified that Bachelor had once worked on a plantation with him, a magistrate granted the slave hunters a certificate to take Bachelor to Maryland.

As luck would have it, the slave hunters—with Bachelor in chains—encountered a doctor named Kinley on the street. Kinley's father had once owned Bachelor and had set him free years earlier. The slave hunters refused to believe this. Kinley went to Isaac Hooper, an abolitionist, with the story of the kidnapped Bachelor. Hooper caught up with Ennells and Frazer and demanded Bachelor's freedom. Ennells drew a pistol and threat-

ened Hooper, but the abolitionist had the law on his side. Ennells eventually agreed to go before another magistrate to prove that Bachelor was an escaped slave. This time Dr. Kinley testified on behalf of the free black man, and Bachelor was finally released.

Members of the Abolition Society decided to bring kidnapping charges against Ennells, but the case was later dismissed. Ennells and Frazer continued their career as slave hunters, no doubt kidnapping any likely suspect that would bring them profit in the South. Breyfogle discussed this issue in *Make Free:*

Even Negroes who were legally free were often made victims of a device commonly used by agents of slave-hunters. This was to send South exact descriptions of Negroes living in the North whom it was intended to kidnap. The descriptions were printed as handbills, to be displayed as proof of ownership when the alleged fugitive was seized and brought before a magistrate. All too often, magistrates found such evidence convincing.[38]

Fighting Back

This is not to say that the work of the slave hunter was safe and easy. Many fugitives were armed, others traveled in groups, and many were willing to die fighting rather than return to a life of slavery. The story of four fugitive slaves in Virginia demonstrates some of the common attitudes of runaways who were confronted by slave catchers.

The two men and two women had stolen their master's wagon and horses and were making their way to Canada in 1855. It was after Christmas, and the biting frost and snow was made worse by the escapees' gnawing hunger and fear. About one hundred miles from home, the runaways were attacked by six white men and a boy who felt it was their duty to return the slaves to their masters. William Still continues the story:

The *spokesman* amongst the fugitives, affecting no ordinary amount of dignity, told their assailants plainly, that "no gentleman would interfere with persons riding along civilly"—not allowing it to be supposed that they were slaves, of course. These "gentlemen," however, were not

Paying Off the Slave Hunters

Most slave hunters were men with little morals or scruples who were willing to hunt, maim, and even kill runaway slaves simply for the reward offered by the masters. In some cases, however, the greed of the hunters worked to the advantage of the fugitives if they—or their friends on the Underground Railroad—could raise enough money to pay off the slave owner's reward to the hunter. Some abolitionists in Austinburg, Ohio, pledged enough money to free a runaway known as Jerry Rescue. The list was printed in the 1896 book *From Dixie to Canada*.

"We whose names are hereto affixed, promise to pay to Eliphalet Austin the sums put to our names, for the purpose of liberating from slavery a colored man whose master is supposed to be in pursuit, and offers to free him for three hundred and fifty dollars.
Austinburg, July 23, 1834

Eliphalet & Aaron E. Austin, $50
J. Austin, $40.00.
J. S. Mills, $2.00.

A. A. Barr, $1.00.
G. W. St. John, $25.00.
Luman Whiting, $2.00.
I. Hendry, $5.00.
Amos Fisk, $5.00.
Daniel Hubbard, $1.00.
Mr. Sawtell, $2.00.
L. M. Austin, $5.00.
Dr. A. Hawley, $2.00.
Ward, $5.00.
Jefferson, $20.00.
Orestes K. Hawley, $50
L. Bissell, $20.00.
T. H. Wells, $3.00.
Harvey Ladd, Jr., $2.00.
James Sillak, $3.00.
Benjamin Whiting, $1.00.
Giddings & Wade, $10.
Russell Clark, $2.00.
Henry Harris, $1.00.
E. Austin, Jr., $15.00.
Ros. Austin, $5.00.
W. Webb, Jr., $5.00.
Henry, $5.00.
A Friend, 50 cents."

willing to accept this account of the travelers. . . . Having the law on their side, they were for compelling the fugitives to surrender without further parley.

At this juncture, the fugitives verily believing that the time had arrived for the practical use of their pistols and dirks, pulled them out of their concealment—the young women as well as the young men—and declared they would not be "taken!" One of the white men raised his gun, pointing the muzzle directly towards one of the young women, with the threat that he would "shoot," etc. "Shoot! shoot!! shoot!!!" she exclaimed, with a double barrelled pistol in one hand and a long dirk knife in the other, utterly unterrified and fully ready for a death struggle. The male *leader* of the fugitives by this time had "pulled back the hammers" of his "pistols" and was about to fire! Their adversaries seeing the weapons, and the unflinching determination on the part of the *runaways* to stand their ground, "spill blood, kill, or die," rather than be "taken," very prudently "sidled over to the other side of the road" leaving . . . the victors to travel on their way.[39]

On another occasion in 1851, a well-organized group of free blacks and escaped slaves fought an organized battle against some well-known slave hunters in Christiana, Pennsylvania. William Breyfogle recorded the story:

The leader of the Negroes was William Parker, himself an escaped slave, who had given shelter and help to many other runaways. On September 10, 1851, the Philadelphia Vigilance Committee sent him word to be on the lookout for slave-hunters. These were led by a Marylander named Gorsuch, who had warrants for two of his slaves known to be staying at Parker's house. Gorsuch, with his son and a band of friends, reached Christiana about daybreak, and unceremoniously broke into Parker's house. By previous arrangement, the defenders blew a horn from an upstairs window, and between fifty and a hundred Negroes, with guns, clubs and corn-knives, came running. Two Quakers, Castner Hanway and Elijah Lewis, had appeared, evidently to try to prevent violence. . . . But the Quakers got no hearing from either side, and the fight began. During its course, Gorsuch was killed, his son seriously wounded, and the two slaves for whom they had warrants escaped.[40]

This "riot" made headlines across the country, and thirty-five blacks, two Quakers, and three whites were arrested and charged with conspiracy to violate the Fugitive Slave Law. Eventually all charges were dropped.

There were victories on both sides of the battle, and there are no records of how many slave hunters were thwarted in their attempts to return fugitive slaves. The odds greatly favored the slave catchers, however, and the penalties meted out to those who were captured were calculated to be severe and cruel.

Punishing the Runaways

Most runaway slaves lived in states that bordered free states. For them, the worst punishment was to be sold to plantations in the Deep South, where treatment of slaves was more barbaric than in border states and where the chances of escape were dim. But this was not the only punishment trackers and slave hunters doled out to their captured victims.

To prevent slaves from running away, some slave owners branded their initials into the flesh of their slaves.

Brutal whippings were a common punishment for captured runaways. Andrew Jackson—who was president of the United States from 1829 to 1837—once offered a $50 reward for the return of a runaway "and ten dollars extra for every hundred lashes any person will give him to the amount of three hundred."[41]

Others were, if possible, even more cruel. One Georgia planter pulled out the toenails of a runaway slave. Some slave owners branded their returned slaves with a hot iron. In an 1852 interview, James Smith, a runaway slave from Virginia, described his ordeal upon return to his slave owner. After being beaten and taken to the cold dungeon of the Richmond jail,

> His master came after him with the spirit of a demon. After having him stripped and most unmercifully flogged, a hot iron was applied to his quivering flesh on one side of his face and back of his neck, which left stamped, in letters of flesh and blood, the initials of his master's name.[42]

Once back on the plantation, runaways were expected to go back to work immediately, even if they had been whipped more than one hundred times and had salt and pepper rubbed into their wounds. The punishments and humiliations did not end there. An 1841 magazine article in the *Anti-Slavery Reporter* described the treatment of a returned fugitive named Madison Jefferson:

> After [his whipping] he was placed in the dark dungeon for two days, and then made to walk up and down before the house in chains, with a bell upon his head, which is fixed in the following manner;—a band of iron goes around the waist with upright bands connecting it with the collar, from whence two other upright pieces terminate in a cross bar, to the centre of which, beyond the reach of the wearer, a bell is suspended; this degrading instrument he wore for several days, and was then sent to the field, being locked up and chained nightly for five or six months,

A few southern states enacted laws that allowed whites to shoot or even kill runaway slaves.

by which time he was supposed to be cured of running away, and had promised on his knees not to repeat the attempt.[43]

North Carolina was one state that allowed the outright murder of "vicious" runaways. For instance, two judges gave notice that a slave named London had committed felonies and other crimes. Unless London surrendered immediately, "any person may KILL and DESTROY the said slave by such means as he or they may think fit, without accusation or impeachment of any crime or offense for so doing."[44]

In Louisiana any white person could shoot a runaway who would not stop on command. The state supreme court cautioned that slave hunters should try to avoid giving a runaway a mortal wound, but if it happened, no penalty would accrue to the slave killer.

Lives of the Conductors

Conductors on the Underground Railroad—both black and white—risked life and limb to move runaway slaves from one station to the next. Some were ex-slaves driven by hatred of the bondage system. Many were Quakers following deeply held religious beliefs. Others were simply common citizens appalled by slavery.

With the enactment of the Fugitive Slave Act in February 1793, aiding runaway slaves became a federal offense. Anyone who harbored an escaped slave or prevented his or her arrest could be fined $500—a considerable sum of money at that time. In 1850, that penalty was boosted to $1,000—a huge amount that would bankrupt almost anyone who was forced to pay it.

Because of this, according to Henrietta Buckmaster in the 1941 book *Let My People Go,*

Conductors learned very early on the advantage of discretion; many times information was conveyed from one friend to another by innuendo so that no names need be mentioned and no information given which could be used against them if arrested.

Buckmaster explains why it was so simple for the Underground Railroad to operate with little formal structure:

When a man emerged from slavery, weak and gasping, a friend opened his door to him, hid him from his pursuers until his fatigue and weakness were past, and then hurried him along in the protection of the night across fields, through woods, over rivers, to the house of the next friend. Or if more than two or three needed help,

A white woman offers her help to a slave contemplating an escape.

loaded them into wagons, and covered them with bags of farm produce, and carried them to the next "station" in the daylight as though merely traveling on his own business. [45]

Some conductors on the Underground Railroad traveled hundreds of miles to help fugitive slaves, while others traveled only ten miles to the next town. Conductors came from all walks of life. Some were wagon drivers who took wagonloads of slaves ten or twelve miles to the next station. Others were steamboat workers who continually smuggled slaves aboard ships. There were brave conductors who traveled deep into the South to provide slaves on plantations with directions for escape. Others personally led slaves through dark forests to freedom in the North.

Some conductors were hardworking farmers who lived in extremely rural areas where there was little chance for excitement or entertainment. In *Make Free*, William

Breyfogle explains that some conductors combined their moral beliefs with the thrill of evading the law and the reward of helping someone in need:

[Let] us begin with an Indiana farmer sitting on his kitchen steps at dusk, after a long day in the fields.

What roused him from a state between sleep and waking was a rustle down at the edge of the corn-patch . . . when he [walked], close to the growing corn, a murmur of low voices began. Two, this time. A man and a woman. Or rather, a boy and a girl, as the farmer saw when they had followed him back to the kitchen. His wife was frying ham and eggs, and he had time to study them, without seeming to. Light-complexioned, and maybe eighteen or nineteen years old. The girl would be worth more, in the South, for her color. Gentlemen of fash-

This house, built in Millfield, Ohio, in 1803, was a travelers' inn that contained secret rooms next to the chimney in the attic where runaway slaves could be hidden.

The Underground Railroad

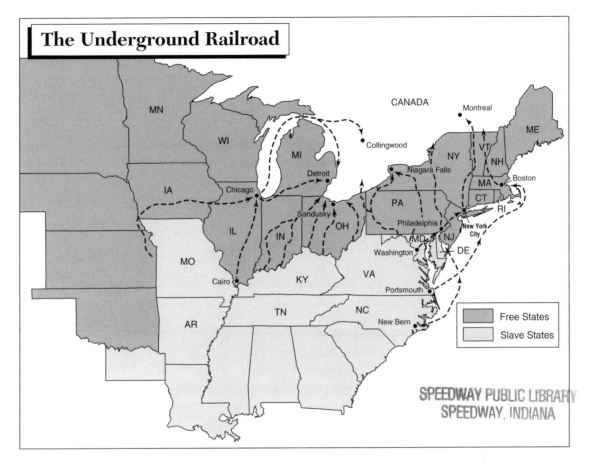

ion in New Orleans had an eye for a girl who could almost pass for white. . . . If it had been just a single man, he could have been given food and directions and sent on to the next station by himself. Now, the farmer had to hitch up and drive twenty miles before he slept.

Oddly, he didn't resent it. The queer little excitement that even a sober, middle-aged man could feel without shame was stealing over him again. . . .

Ten miles to the north, the next station-keeper would keep them hidden all day and set them forward on their way the next night. For his part, the farmer would come back just before dawn and cut two more notches on the post in the stable where he kept his records. The horses knew the road back well by now, and often he got a few winks of sleep on the way back.[46]

Runaway slaves escaped across fields, valleys, forests, and mountain slopes. Conductors escorted them between states and showed them stations in a variety of places, from unused chicken coops to beautiful mansions in Boston. The routes may not have been the most direct, but they were generally considered safe by the conductors.

As a free state bordered by two slave states, Ohio was geographically located in the center of much Underground Railroad activity.

Lives of the Conductors **51**

There were multiple places a conductor could help a runaway cross the Ohio River. In southern Ohio alone, there were five families who helped thousands of fugitives make their way to Canada before 1817. Settlers in northern Ohio also shared antislavery sentiment and conducted slaves to safety. Once slaves reached Lake Erie, they found Underground Railroad captains who were willing to sail them to Canada on what came to be known as "abolition boats."

Farther to the west, many escape routes through Indiana and Illinois opened up after 1820. Those who escaped through Indiana were conducted to Michigan, then into Canada. Those who made it to Illinois were taken into Wisconsin, then across Lake Michigan by boat. Earlier conductors followed river routes, and later the Illinois Central Railroad offered another line to freedom.

In the east, one route took passengers from Washington to New York City, then to Albany, then into Canada via Syracuse and Rochester. Conductors also led slaves through New England and by boat along the coasts of New Hampshire and Maine, and finally into Canada.

Spiriting slaves away from slave hunters—and the law—required bravery, intelligence, and skill. There were many—estimated to be 3,211 people—who acted as conductors and stationmasters on the Underground Railroad. Each one used his or her own methods to gain freedom for the oppressed. According to Wilbur Siebert in the definitive 1898 book *The Underground Railroad from Slavery to Freedom,*

> Considering the kind of labor performed and the danger involved, one is impressed with the unselfish devotion to principle of these emancipators. There was for them, no course, no outward honor, no material recompense, but instead [if they were caught] such . . . disgrace as can scarcely be comprehended.

> Nevertheless, they were rich in courage, and their hospitality was equal to all emergencies. They gladly gave aid and comfort to every negro seeking freedom; and the numbers befriended by many helpers despite penalties and abuse show with what moral determination the work was carried on.[47]

Tricks of the Conductor Trade

To outwit the skillful slave hunters, conductors often used deception to help those in need. Female conductors formed sewing circles with names like the Anti-Slavery Sewing Society to make elaborate disguises for runaways. Fugitives could travel the railroad dressed as riverboat hands, railroad workers, nurses, nannies, or other occupations. Sometimes runaways simply carried scythes, rakes, or other farm tools so that they looked like farmers instead of fugitives. Sometimes light-skinned slaves might blacken their faces and hands with burnt cork so that their skin appeared much darker than the description given of them. As Wilbur Siebert wrote,

> [The Rev. Calvin] Fairbanks tells us that he piloted slave-girls in the finery of ladies, men and boys tricked out as gentlemen and the servants of gentlemen; and that sometimes he found it necessary to require his followers to don the garments of the opposite sex. In May, 1843, Mr. Fairbanks went to Arkansas for the purpose of rescuing William Minnis from bondage. He found that the slave was a young black man of light complexion and

[handsome] appearance, and that he closely resembled a [white] gentleman living in the vicinity of Little Rock. Minnis was, therefore, fitted out with the necessary wig, beard and mustache, and clothes like those of his model; he was quickly drilled in the deportment of his assumed rank; and, as the test proved, he sustained himself well in his part. On boarding the boat that was to carry him to freedom he discovered his owner, Mr. Brennan, but so effectual was the slave's make-up that the master failed to penetrate the disguise.[48]

It was a common trick to dress fugitives as the opposite sex. Levi Coffin, who sheltered thousands of runaway slaves, describes how he helped a large group of slaves pass directly under the watchful eyes of the slave hunters:

A close watch was kept on every road leading out of the city, and the friends of the fugitives dared not move them in any direction for more than a week. At last we hit upon a plan to get them out in disguise, in open daylight. The males were disguised as females, and the females as males, and thus attired they were seated in elegant carriages, and driven out of the city at different points, exactly at noon, when most people were at [lunch]. Those who were on the look-out for a company of frightened, poorly dressed fugitives, did not recognize the objects of their search, for it was quite common for the colored gentry to go out riding in that style.[49]

Female fugitives, when not disguised as men, were sometimes dressed in the modest outfits commonly worn by Quaker women. Veiled bonnets covered their face and hair, long dresses covered their legs, and gloves covered the hands.

There were many slaves in border states who helped runaways who passed throughout their territory. In Baltimore, two free African American women who sold produce at the

Female conductors formed sewing circles to create disguises for fugitive slaves.

street market also secretly worked for the Vigilance Committee of Philadelphia conducting slaves north. Frederick Douglass's connection with the Underground Railroad began long before he left the South. In the North, almost every city with more than ten thousand people was home to a community of African Americans who became enthusiastic workers for the railroad. Black settlements in the free states and along the southern frontier became an important part of the chain of stations leading to Canada.

Richard Daly, who was born in Trimble County, Kentucky, on a plantation on the Ohio River, was a slave who acted as a conductor on the Underground Railroad. Daly was the property of Samuel and George Ferrin, two brothers who were kind men and who treated Daly well. Although Daly often went to the market in Madison, Indiana—a free state—and had ample opportunity for escape, he did not care to leave. Daly was married to a slave named Kitty who lived on a

Fugitives often donned clothing commonly worn by Quakers, shown here, which covered their faces, legs, and hands.

nearby plantation. The couple had four children, so Daly chose to remain on the Ferrins' plantation.

Because Daly lived on the northernmost edge of the slave state of Kentucky, he acted as a conductor on the Underground Railroad.

> I had for years belonged to the underground railroad, and had helped about thirty slaves to escape. They would come from some of the counties in Kentucky back of the [Green River], and send word to me beforehand. I would meet them about two miles above Milton, Ky., on the river bank at night and row them over in a boat. I would fire my revolver when I was crossing the Ohio River, and my white friend, who was an agent of the underground railroad, would fire his revolver to say he was ready. Then I would land the fugitives, and he would take care of them and pass them along the road to Canada.[50]

Daly eventually ran away when his wife died at the age of twenty during childbirth. The owner of Daly's children planned to sell one of them, so the conductor became a fugitive himself, taking his children with him.

Conductor Harriet Tubman

Harriet Tubman, known as the "Moses of Her People," was an escaped slave herself and the most famous conductor on the railroad. Tubman was born around 1821 in Dorchester County, Maryland, and escaped from slavery in 1849. She made her way ninety miles on foot to Philadelphia, where she worked by day as a cook in a hotel. At night, Tubman attended meetings of the Philadelphia Vigilance Committee.

Escaped slave Harriet Tubman guided hundreds of slaves to freedom, becoming a legendary figure on the Underground Railroad.

After she had successfully escaped, Tubman occasionally heard news about her parents and brothers and sisters who were still living in bondage in Maryland. When she heard that her sister Mary and her children were about to be sold, possibly to a plantation farther south, Tubman volunteered to go rescue them. Ignoring warnings from other committee members that it was too dangerous a mission for a fugitive slave, Tubman traveled to Baltimore to guide her sister and her family from station to station until they reached Philadelphia. The success of the mission gave her courage to rescue other family members.

In the autumn of 1851, dressed like a man in a suit and hat, Tubman made her way back to the plantation she had first run away from. She found her brother John and his wife, but they were too afraid to leave. Instead Tubman moved quietly through the plantation slave quarters knocking on doors. Soon she had collected a small group of slaves who desired their freedom and successfully navigated the long trek to Philadelphia.

Tubman returned to the South in December 1851 on another rescue mission. By this time, word had spread of her bravery, people were calling her Moses, and she was quickly becoming a legend among the slaves. Again, Tubman conducted a group north, traveling by night and hiding by day. They scaled mountains, forded rivers, and threaded their way through dense woodlands, hiding when pursuers passed them. Babies were given an opium-laced medicine called paregoric to keep them from crying. According to her 1869 biography, *Harriet Tubman: The Moses of Her People*, Tubman conducted her fugitives through the worst sort of terrain to escape detection:

> [There] was a little island in a swamp, where grass grew tall and rank, and where no human being could be suspected of seeking a hiding place. To this spot she conducted her party; she waded the swamp, carrying in a basket two well-drugged babies . . . and the rest of the company following. She ordered them to lie down in the tall, wet, grass, and here she prayed again, and waited for deliverance. The poor creatures were all cold, wet, and hungry, and Harriet did not dare leave them to get supplies.[51]

On her second rescue mission, Tubman conducted eleven slaves to freedom, including another brother and his wife. Because a new influx of slave hunters was quickly making Philadelphia unsafe for fugitive slaves, Tubman

Religious Background of White Conductors

Many white people who acted as conductors operated out of deeply held religious beliefs. Of all the white religious sects, Quakers protested slavery for the longest period of time. According to *The Underground Railroad from Slavery to Freedom*, as early as 1688, Pennsylvania Quakers, also known as the "Religious Society of Friends," protested "against the traffic in the bodies of men and the treatment of men as cattle."

By the eighteenth century, Quakers began to expel members from the church if they owned slaves. In the nineteenth century, Quaker committees in the South examined laws in free states respecting the admission of runaway slaves. They determined that there was "nothing in the laws of Ohio, Indiana, and Illinois to prevent the introduction of people of color into those states, and [conductors] were instructed to remove slaves placed in their care as fast as they were willing to go." As a result, many Quakers who lived in the South hated slavery so much that they moved north and established important Underground Railroad routes.

Methodists began to take action against slavery in 1785 when they adopted a resolution that prohibited "'The buying or selling the bodies or souls of men, women, or children, with the intention to enslave them.' In 1816, [Methodist leaders] adopted the resolution that 'no slaveholder shall be eligible to any official station in our Church hereafter.'"

The third religious sect to which many conductors belonged was Presbyterianism. In 1818 the church declared the system of slavery to be "inconsistent with the law of God and totally irreconcilable with the gospel."

There were, of course, people of other religious faiths who helped fugitive slaves, but it was much easier for a large effort like the Underground Railroad to be organized by trusted members of the same church or the same religion.

---

took this large group all the way to St. Catharines in Ontario, Canada. Since it was late December and snow was falling, Tubman decided she could not abandon the ex-slaves. She and the others got jobs to pay rent on a small house and to put food on the table. Tubman was amazed by Canada, where black men could vote, hold office, sit on juries, and live wherever they chose. She decided to move to St. Catharines, and she based her operations out of that city for many years.

From 1852 to 1857, the woman called Moses returned twice a year to Maryland to bring out slaves—once in the spring and once in the fall. Between trips Tubman worked in hotels to raise money. Almost everyone she helped was a stranger to her. Tubman had an uncanny ability to sense when danger was near, and she was able to persuade hundreds of frightened fugitives to endure heat, cold, hunger, and fatigue in order to find freedom.

Slaveholders eventually offered a $40,000 reward for Tubman. This added a new element of danger to her operations. When individuals faltered or fell behind on rescue missions, Tubman refused to let them return to their plantations and risk capture for the entire group. Moses was quick to pull out her pistol and threaten those who dared turn around. As Sarah Bradford wrote in *Harriet Tubman: The Moses of Her People,*

The way was so toilsome over the rugged mountain passes, that often the *men* who followed her would give out, and foot-sore, and bleeding, they would drop on the ground, groaning that they could not take another step. They would lie there and die, or if strength came back, they would return on their steps, and seek their old homes again. Then the revolver carried by this bold and daring pioneer [Tubman], would come out, while pointing it at their heads she would say, "Dead niggers tell no tales; you go on or die!" And by this heroic treatment she compelled them to drag their weary limbs along on their northward journey.[52]

By 1858 Tubman had conducted more than three hundred slaves to freedom, including her aged parents. Tubman's operation was so successful that there were parts of Maryland where the entire slave population had made its escape, causing a general panic among slaveholders in the region. In December 1860, Tubman led her final group of runaways to freedom. The Civil War soon broke out, and Tubman served as a spy and a guide for the Union army in Maryland and Virginia. After the war, she managed a home for elderly blacks in Auburn, New York, until her death at the age of ninety-two in 1913. Tubman was buried with full military honors.

How Many Were Offered Help

Conductors on the Underground Railroad were tight-lipped about how many fugitive slaves they helped. That is understandable, because if they were fined $1,000 apiece by courts for every slave they helped, some would have owed more than a million dollars. In 1898 Wilbur Siebert compiled a partial list of conductors and the numbers of fugitives that they helped. Siebert wrote that only five families in southern Ohio helped more than one thousand runaways get to Canada. Daniel Gibbons of Lancaster County, Pennsylvania, was a conductor for more than fifty-six years. "He did not keep a record of the number he passed until 1824. But prior to that time, it was supposed to have been over 200, and up to the time of his death (in 1853) he had aided about 1,000," Siebert writes. Another man, Dr. Nathan M. Thomas of Schoolcraft, Michigan, helped between 1,000 and 1,500 fugitives. Siebert continues,

With her trunk packed with antislavery literature, a young woman decides to join the abolitionist movement.

William Still and the Vigilance Committee

William Still was a well-known Underground Railroad agent and conductor. He was born free in New Jersey, but his parents had been fugitive slaves and bore the psychological scars of bondage. Still devoted his life to assisting other runaways and was so successful that nineteen out of every twenty fugitive slaves passing through Philadelphia stopped at his station.

Still served as a clerk in the Pennsylvania Anti-Slavery Society and as secretary of the Philadelphia Vigilance Committee. He offered help to famous fugitives such as Harriet Tubman, Henry "Box" Brown, and others. In addition to his Underground Railroad activities, Still founded the first black YMCA and was a successful businessman who owned a coal and lumber business.

In 1872, Still wrote the definitive book *The Underground Rail Road*, containing more than 800 pages of his personal accounts, detailing the stories of escaped slaves and Underground Railroad workers.

Still's records are among the few that were hidden—rather than destroyed—after the passage of the Fugitive Slave Law of 1850.

Social reformer William Still devoted his life to helping fugitive slaves.

The Rev. Charles T. Torrey went to Maryland and "from there sent—as he wrote previous to 1844—some 400 slaves over different routes to Canada." Philo Carpenter, of Chicago, is reported to have escorted 200 fugitives to vessels bound for Canada. In a letter to William Still, in November, 1857, Elijah E. Pennypacker, of Chester County, Pennsylvania, writes, "we have within the past two months passed forty-three through our hands." H. B. Leeper, of Princeton, Illinois, says that the most successful business he ever accomplished in this line was the helping on of thirty-one men and women in six weeks' time. Leverett B. Hill, of Wakeman, Ohio, assisted 103 on their way to Canada during the year 1852. Mr. Van Dorn, of Quincy, in a service of twenty-five years, assisted "some two or three hundred fugitives." W. D. Schooley, of Richmond, Indiana, writes, "I think I must have assisted over 100 on their way to liberty.". . . . "Thousands of fugitives found rest" at Ripley, Brown County, Ohio.[53]

Stations and Stationmasters

Many men and women who were conductors on the Underground Railroad also offered their homes as stations. Others acted only as stationmasters and provided food, clothing, shelter, and medical care for fugitive slaves.

Maps of the Underground Railroad show many stations in Illinois, Indiana, Ohio, Pennsylvania, Delaware, New York, Connecticut, Massachusetts, Vermont, and other New England states. Stations within individual states were usually about twelve miles apart—the distance a healthy adult could travel on foot in one night or the distance a wagon carrying several escapees could easily travel from dusk to dawn.

Some stations, such as the one belonging to Levi and Catherine Coffin in Newport, Indiana (later renamed Fountain City), were so well known that three different routes converged at their home. The Coffins, who were Quakers, were so successful as stationmasters that Levi Coffin earned the unofficial title of "President of the Underground Railroad."

Famous Underground Railroad Stations

There were as many different kinds of stations as there were routes through the nineteenth-century American countryside. Slaves were hidden in attics, barns, and cellars. Some stations had secret rooms, hidden closets, trapdoors, and tunnels where runaways could hide.

Several houses were built for the express purpose of hiding fugitive slaves. The Tallman House built in Janesville, Wisconsin, in 1855 contained twenty rooms with hiding places in the attic and basement and a hidden lookout on the roof. The cellar door was always left open, and slaves entered any time, day or night. Upon leaving, the runaways were led through a secret stairwell into an underground tunnel that led to the banks of the Rock River. There, the fugitives boarded a steamboat bound for the town of Milton.

In Milton, the fugitives would hide in the Stagecoach Inn. The Stagecoach Inn

Stationmaster Levi Coffin was commonly known as the president of the Underground Railroad.

was operated by Joshua Goodrich, who dug a tunnel from the inn to a log cabin, out back. Runaways arrived at the cabin, then dropped through a trapdoor into the tunnel, which led to a hiding place in the basement of the inn.

Several of the thousands of Underground Railroad depots that once dotted the American landscape remain standing today. Many of those are African American churches where free blacks organized to help their brethren in bondage. The Mt. Zion United African Methodist Episcopal (A.M.E.) Church in Washington, D.C., was an important point on the road to Canada; fugitive slaves were hidden in the burial vault in the church's cemetery. In New York City, the Mother Zion A.M.E. Church, the oldest African American church in New York State, holds the distinction of having sheltered hundreds of runaways since it was built in 1800.

The Mother Bethel A.M.E. Church in Philadelphia, built in 1805, sat on what is today the oldest piece of real estate in America owned continuously by African Americans. This church was a major station on the Underground Railroad where large sums of money were raised to comfort the fugitives who were sheltered there. Many famed abolitionists spoke there, including Harriet Tubman and Frederick Douglass.

In addition to Quakers and Methodists, people of other religions helped hide fugitive slaves. The Jewish members of the Touro Synagogue in Newport, Rhode Island, sheltered many fugitives who were heading to

How Levi Coffin Got His Nickname

Although there was no official leader of the Underground Railroad, Levi Coffin, who sheltered thousands of fugitive slaves, was commonly known as the president of the Underground Railroad. Henrietta Buckmaster describes how Coffin got his nickname in the book *Let My People Go*.

"It was a Southerner who first called Levi Coffin 'The President of the Underground Railroad.' It came about when seventeen fugitives . . . escaped [together] from Kentucky. They lived through perils . . . and finally reached the Underground Railroad north of the [Ohio] river. Seventeen flight-marked slaves filed into the Coffin kitchen late one night, brought in two wagons by conductors. Seventeen thousand dollars' worth of property sat at a long table and ate the breakfast that was hastily prepared. Early the next morning after the wagons had rumbled on, a message came to Coffin, saying that fifteen Kentuckians had arrived in the neighborhood, hell-bent on [finding] their property. Coffin sent the messenger as fast as he could ride to intercept the wagons and scatter the fugitives. Then he settled down to observe the antics of the catchers. . . .

The hunters hung about the town, refusing to believe that such tangible objects as seventeen slaves would not pass before their eyes if they looked hard enough. Their threats diminished as their prospects waned, and after some weeks they set out for home. As they passed the plain square home of Levi Coffin, they . . . put it into words, 'There's an Underground Railroad around here and Levi Coffin is president.'

This was repeated so often and spread so far that letters came to Newport, addressed to 'Levi Coffin, President of the Underground Railroad.'"

This plaque adorns an 1821 New Jersey home that once served as a station on the Underground Railroad.

Canada and acted as agents and conductors on the Underground Railroad.

In the nineteenth century, northern free blacks built their own villages in the American wilderness to escape prejudice. The town of Timbuktu, New Jersey (now known as Bukto), was one such community, founded in 1820. Named after the fabled city in West Africa, Timbuktu was known as a haven for runaway slaves. Because of its location in an area of dense forests, fugitives felt safe there—until 1860 when a posse of slave hunters attacked the town in what became known as the "Battle of Pine Swamp." The slave hunters were beaten back, and Timbuktu's reputation grew as escaped slaves settled there.

Other railroad depots were known for their odd or unusual hiding places. The D. B. Cole House in Lumberton, New Jersey, employed a false underground water well under the carriage house that was reached by sliding down a chute. Under the well, a room (which can still be seen today) had an arched ceiling reaching twenty feet in height. The House of Many Stairs in the village of Pennsdale, Pennsylvania, was the subject of many fantastic tales. The imposing structure, once known as

Bull's Tavern, also served as a stagecoach stop. Owner Edward Morris offered food, drink, and sleeping rooms to his many customers. The many people coming and going helped stationmaster Morris shield those who might be runaways. If slave hunters arrived, fugitives could disappear down any of the seven stairways in the house. The complex series of stairs led to a small room that was concealed behind paneling where slaves could remain hidden.

In Woodstock, Vermont, the home of Titus Hutchinson employed a tunnel extending for half a mile from the house to the Kedron River. The use of this home as a depot is unusual because Hutchinson was a former chief justice of the Vermont Supreme Court.

Because runaways usually traveled at night, they needed signals to find stations. Sometimes a lantern with a special shade hung in a barn window. In some parts of Vermont, chimneys were fitted with patterned white brick as a welcoming sign. One woman put a flag in the hand of a statue in front of her house when it was safe to enter.

Although the fugitive slave laws threatened expensive fines and jail time for those who harbored runaways, more wearing was the abuse heaped on stationmasters by their

A group of fugitives makes the dangerous trek to the next stop on the Underground Railroad.

neighbors who supported slavery. For many years the abolitionists were in a minority in most communities. They were insulted and taunted by their neighbors who "did not distinguish between abolition of slavery and fusion of the white and black races."[54] Those who harbored runaways were often accused of using the labor of fugitives during harvest time, then hurrying them off with no pay when their services were no longer needed. In fact, many runaways were so grateful for the hospitality of the stationmasters that they offered to work for free to repay their generosity.

Even in villages where a majority of people were against slavery, not everyone was willing to offer help to fugitives. In *Reminiscences of Levi Coffin*, the author describes his neighbors' feelings when his home became a popular stop on the Underground Railroad:

In the winter of 1826–27, fugitives began to come to our house, and as it became more widely known on different routes that the slaves fleeing from bondage would find a welcome and shelter at our house, and be forwarded safely on their journey, the number increased. Friends in the neighborhood, who had formerly stood aloof from the work, fearful of the penalty of the law, were encouraged to engage in it when they saw the fearless manner in which I acted, and the success that attended my efforts. They would contribute to clothe the fugitives, and would aid in forwarding them on their way, but were timid about sheltering them under their roof; so that part of the work [fell] to us. Some seemed really glad to see the work go on, if somebody else would do it. Others doubted the propriety of it, and tried to discourage me, and dissuade me from running such risks. They manifested great concern for my safety and [financial] interests, telling me that such a course of action would injure my business and perhaps ruin me; that I ought to consider the welfare of my family; and warning me that my life was in danger, as there were many threats made against me by the slave-hunters and those who sympathized with them.[55]

When confronted with these arguments, Coffin replied that the Bible told him to feed the hungry and clothe the naked and said nothing about the color of one's skin. And as far as financial interests were concerned, Coffin was a successful merchant and was able to dedicate a good percentage of his money to the "heavy expenses" of maintaining an underground railroad station.

However, Coffin's neighbors were right to be fearful of slave hunters. Stationmasters were often subject to spying by pro-slavery factions. When a large group of blacks arrived at a house, it would obviously arouse suspicion and cause the station to become closely watched. In small, isolated towns, it was extremely difficult for those who were helping slaves to escape notice from their often prying neighbors. Most times, stationmasters were left alone, but in several cases, they were turned in by pro-slave neighbors.

Stationmasters also had to thwart slave hunters who were relentless in the hunt for their prey. These men were inquisitive and vigilant and would spend days watching suspected activities at stations. To find their quarry, they had only to report the stationmasters to the local police. Many houses in well-traveled areas of the railroad were under constant surveillance by slave hunters. Towns and villages in regions adjacent to southern states were often terrorized by crowds of rowdy slave hunters eager to find hidden slaves.

A letter written in 1843 by William Steel details how one northern Ohio county was invaded by slave hunters from Virginia.

The abolitionists of the west part of [Monroe] county have had very difficult work in getting [the runaways] off without being caught, as the whole of that part of the county has been filled with Southern blood hounds upon their track, and some of the abolitionists' houses have been watched day and night for several days in succession. This evening a company of eight Virginia hounds passed through this place north on the hunt of some of their two-legged chattels. . . . Since writing the above I have understood that something near twenty Virginians including the eight above mentioned have just passed through town.[56]

Station Operations

For those who operated stations on the Underground Railroad, barely a week went by when they were not roused from bed in the middle of the night by a gentle rap at the door. Since Quakers, known as "Friends," often acted as stationmasters, passengers would announce their arrival with the statement that it was "a Friend with friends."

The door would open and the group would enter the station without a word, for they never knew who might be watching and listening, even at such a late hour. With all safely inside, and the door securely locked, the stationmaster then pulled heavy curtains over the windows and finally struck a warming fire.

Acting out of deeply held religious beliefs, Quakers often served as stationmasters on the Underground Railroad.

By this time, the stationmaster's spouse would be awake and offering help. Soup was heated and bread pulled from the cupboard, and within a short time, the cold, hungry fugitives would be made comfortable. The stationmaster might accompany the conductor to the stable and care for the tired horses that had, perhaps, run twenty-five or thirty miles that night through the inclement weather. Back inside the house, the fugitives were able to find peaceful sleep on straw-covered pallets before the fireplace.

On some evenings, two or three parties with no knowledge of one another might converge in one station. On nights like these, the stationmaster would repeat the same chores for up to twenty people. Levi Coffin writes about such hectic nights:

The care of so many necessitated much work and anxiety on our part, but we as-sumed the burden of our own will and bore it cheerfully. It was never too cold or stormy, or the hour of night too late for my wife to rise from sleep, and provide food and comfortable lodging for the fugitives. Her sympathy for those in distress never tired, and her efforts in their behalf never abated. This work was kept up during the time we lived in Newport, a period of more than twenty years.

Coffin maintained that he helped an average of more than one hundred fugitives a year, and the work required more than simply providing food and a place to sleep for the runaways:

They generally came to us destitute of clothing, and were often barefooted. Clothing must be collected and kept on hand, if possible and money must be

Living Under Constant Threat

With the price of slaves running anywhere from $400 to $2,500, stationmasters on the Underground Railroad lived under constant threat of retaliation from slave owners and hunters for hiding their "property." Levi Coffin wrote about the dangers he faced daily in his 1876 book *Reminiscences of Levi Coffin.*

"[Slave hunters] often threatened to kill me, and at various times offered a reward for my head. I often received anonymous letters warning me that my store, pork-house, and dwelling would be burned to the ground, and one letter, mailed in Kentucky, informed me that a body of armed men were then on their way to Newport to destroy the town. The letter named the night in which the work would be accomplished, and warned me to flee from the place for if I should be taken my life would pay for my crimes against Southern slaveholders. I had become so accustomed to threats and warnings, that this made no impression on me, struck no terror to my heart. The most of the inhabitants of our village were Friends [Quakers], and their principles were those of peace and non-resistance. They were not alarmed at the threat to destroy the town, and on the night appointed retired to their beds as usual and slept peacefully. We placed no sentinels to give warning of danger, and had no extra company at our house to guard our lives. . . . In the morning our buildings were all there—there was no smell of fire, no sign of the terrible destruction threatened."

Aside from arriving cold, tired, and hungry, those traveling the Underground Railroad in the winter would often arrive at stations with severe frostbite.

raised to buy shoes, and purchase goods to make garments for women and children. The young ladies in the neighborhood organized a sewing society, and met at our house frequently, to make clothes for the fugitives.[57]

This lack of clothing could have serious consequences. In cold temperatures, runaways would arrive at stations with severe frostbite. Coffin wrote about one pair of runaways who arrived in an early winter cold spell. The fugitives' feet were so frozen that they were unable to walk for three months. A sympathetic doctor treated them and their feet were saved from amputation. One of the runaways was so grateful that he returned to

Coffin's home the next year and offered to work for him to repay him.

Sometimes fugitive slaves were required to hide in stations for days, weeks, or even months at a time. In such situations, the runaways would be concealed in attics, basements, or secret rooms. Levi Coffin describes how he sheltered runaways for weeks at a time with no one the wiser.

Our house was large and well adapted for secreting fugitives. Very often slaves would lie concealed in upper chambers for weeks without the boarders or frequent visitors at the house knowing anything about it. My wife had a quiet unconcerned way of going about her work as if nothing unusual was on hand, which was calculated to lull every suspicion of those who might be watching and who would have been at once aroused by any sign of secrecy or mystery. Even the intimate friends of the family did not know when there were slaves hidden in the house, unless they were directly informed. When my wife took food to the fugitives she generally concealed it in a basket, and put some freshly ironed garment on the top to make it look like a basket full of clean clothes. Fugitives were not often allowed to eat in the kitchen, from fear of detection.[58]

The Trials and Tribulations of Thomas Garrett

Thomas Garrett was another famous stationmaster, who was remembered in story and song for his bravery in Wilmington, Delaware. Born a Pennsylvania Quaker in 1789, Garrett harbored an intense hatred for the institution of slavery. For almost four decades, the stationmaster sheltered at least twenty-seven hundred slaves with the help of Wilmington's African American community. Although his house was under constant surveillance, Garrett managed to elude the law for many years.

Garrett was brave and proud and refused to be intimidated. When he heard that the state of Maryland was offering a $10,000 reward for his capture, he wrote an open letter to a newspaper claiming that he was worth at least $20,000 and that if anyone would pay that much, Garrett would collect the reward himself. Threats of murder were so common that a group of his free black comrades established a watch at his front door and took turns guarding him at night.

In 1848, after Garrett had been helping runaways for twenty-six years, the law caught up with him. This was during a time when the powerful slave states were eager to stem the flow of fugitives north and make an example of abolitionists who assisted them. Garrett was put on trial under the pretext of having aided two runaway slaves, found guilty, and assessed damages of $5,400—"fined so heavily that he was left without a cent."[59] Henrietta Buckmaster described Garrett's reaction:

When his sentence had been pronounced, he rose in the courtroom, a tall rather stooping old figure with white hair, soft as a baby's, and drooping lids that did not conceal the fire that suddenly blazed in his eyes. "Judge," he said, "now that thee hast relieved me of what little I possessed, I will go home and put another story on my house. I want room to accommodate more of God's poor." After a bare glance at him Garrett turned to the courtroom and for an hour expounded on the evils of slavery. He spared no one. He spoke . . . as men seldom had the courage to speak. . . . When at length he sat down, breathing only a little more deeply than when he had begun, one of the jurors who had convicted him ran across the courtroom and seized his hand. "Give me your forgiveness," he said, "and let me be your friend." "Freely given," said Garrett . . . "if thee cease to be an advocate of the [immoral] system of slavery."

Everything was sold. He watched his household goods and his merchandise carried out to the auctioneer. When the sale was over the auctioneer turned to him and said with a glint of righteousness, "Thomas, I hope you'll never be caught at this again." Only as quickly as it took him

Native American Rescuers

Although Native Americans were not considered "stationmasters" or "conductors" on the Underground Railroad, many did help harbor runaway slaves. Wilbur Siebert offers details in *The Underground Railroad from Slavery to Freedom*.

"In the early days running slaves sometimes sought and received aid from Indians. This fact is evidenced by the introduction of fugitive recovery clauses into a number of the treaties made between the colonies and Indian tribes. Seven out of the eight treaties made between 1784 and 1786 contained clauses for the return of black prisoners, or of 'negroes and other property.' A few of the colonies offered rewards to induce Indians to apprehend and restore runaways.... The inhabitants of the Ottawa village of Chief Kinjeino in northwestern Ohio were kindly disposed towards the fugitive; and the people of Chief Brant, who held an estate on the Grand River in Ontario west of Niagara Falls, were in the habit of receiving colored refugees."

to put the words together, Garrett answered, "Friend, I haven't a dollar in the world, but if thee knows a fugitive who needs a breakfast, send him to me."[60]

Garrett remade his life at sixty, became successful in business, and bought back many of the items that had been auctioned off by the government. True to his promise, Garrett built an extra story on his house to harbor fugitives. His trial brought him fame, and his name was spread among slaves in the deepest South. Runaways came in greater numbers, and contributions poured in from sympathizers to help Garrett rebuild his life. Harriet Tubman often stopped at his home seeking food, shelter, and money while leading fugitives to Canada. As time passed, Garrett became "an Abolitionist in the fullest sense: a champion of women's rights, an advocate of temperance, a defender of the Indians, and an agitator in behalf of white working men and women."[61]

CHAPTER 6

Building New Lives in Canada

Before the Fugitive Slave Law of 1850, runaway slaves only needed to escape to the free northern states to begin new lives. But once they reached New York City, Cleveland, Philadelphia, Hartford, and elsewhere, they found that running away was only the beginning of their new struggle. Most fugitives had few job skills, could not read or write, and found little work open to them. Blacks were turned away from dining in restaurants and denied access to schools and churches. Public transportation was segregated, and hotels closed their doors to blacks. Although they were free to do as they pleased, that also meant they were free to starve.

Many ex-slaves thought that they would receive better treatment in Canada, and even before the Fugitive Slave Act, thousands of southern blacks pressed on past America's northern border. After the Fugitive Slave Law was enacted, the numbers of blacks leaving the United States rose dramatically. In 1852, the Anti-Slavery Society of Canada estimated the black population of Canada to be thirty

Many former slaves found life difficult in the northern states, where they faced discrimination and limited job opportunities.

Thousands of slaves trekked to Canada, hoping to receive better treatment there than they had received in the United States.

thousand. Nearly all of those people were fugitive slaves from the United States. By the time of the Civil War in 1861, Canada's black population had swelled to forty-five thousand fugitives and fifteen thousand freeborn people of African descent.

Canada had been a refuge for runaway slaves as early as 1705 when the French flag flew over the country. But when the English took over Canada in 1763, slavery was legalized. Canada's attitude toward slavery, however, soon changed. According to Horatio T. Strother's *The Underground Railroad in Connecticut,*

> [The] American Revolution soon followed [in 1776]; in Canadian eyes the United States had become an enemy country, and enemy property would not readily be returned. Within twenty years thereafter slavery was ended in Canada

by a series of court decisions, holding that the air of this British land was "too pure for a slave to breathe."

This made Canada more than ever the refugees' goal, and before the War of 1812 reached its inconclusive end, the words "Canada" and "freedom" were used interchangeably by slaves in all the shanties and quarters in the South.[62]

Black Settlers in Canadian Towns

Most of the fugitive slaves escaped to what is today the Canadian province of Ontario and what was then known as Canada West. Those who crossed from Ohio and Michigan settled on a long finger of land with Lake Huron to the north and Lake Erie to the south. There

Lies Told to Slaves About Canada

It was in the best interests of southern slave-holders to get slaves to believe that Canada was a frozen wasteland where African Americans could never survive. In *Slave Testimony*, Joseph Smith, born a slave in Maryland in 1814, remembered what white Southerners had told him about Canada.

"I stopped in Jersey State some six or seven years before I came to Canada, & there is where I got intelligence about Canada. The white people at the South said nobody could live here; that they had no horses here, no hogs, & no cows, and all such stuff as that—

that they didn't raise anything here much at all. Well, I always made them believe that I didn't care anything about Canada or any other free State. And so, some five years after that, they got some wild goose wheat, that was called 'Canada Wheat,' and I said—'I thought they couldn't raise anything in Canada. How did this wheat grow there?' 'Why, it was upon a warm, ridgy place,' they said; 'that's how it came to grow there.'"

Smith escaped to Canada in 1842, bought his own farm, and acquired "some considerable personal property, besides real estate."

they moved into the cities of Windsor, Chatham, and London. Those who came across from Buffalo, New York, tended to stay in St. Catharines, Hamilton, Toronto, and other cities bordering Lake Ontario. In the city of St. Catharines, about eight hundred blacks lived among a population of six thousand. "The houses occupied by the colored people are neat and plain without; tidy and comfortable within,"[63] wrote Benjamin Drew.

The 1856 book *A North-Side View of Slavery* expressed these hopeful words regarding St. Catharines (which was sometimes spelled "St. Catherines"):

REFUGE! Refuge for the oppressed! Refuge for Americans escaping from the abuse and cruel bondage in their native land! Refuge for my countrymen from the lash of the overseer, from the hounds and guns of southern man-hunters, from the clutches of northern marshals and commissioners! Rest! Rest for the hunted slave! Rest for the travel-soiled and foot-sore fugitive.

Refuge and Rest! These are the first ideas which arise in my mind in connection with the town of St. Catherines.[64]

In Toronto, about one thousand blacks lived in a city of forty-seven thousand. Benjamin Drew writes: "Many of the colored people own the houses in which they dwell, and some have acquired valuable estates. . . . A portion of them sustain a . . . debating club (which is attended by both sexes) where debates are held, and original essays are read."[65]

The town of Galt contained about three thousand people. According to escaped slave William Thompson, "There are in Galt about forty colored people. As a general thing, they are more industrious, frugal, and temperate than the whites."[66]

The larger city of London had a population of 12,000, 350 of whom were fugitive slaves. "Some of the latter are among the most intelligent and respected citizens; but others do not improve their time and opportunities as they ought,"[67] Drew writes.

"At [the town of] Chatham," said Mr. John Little, "the fugitives are as thick as blackbirds in a corn-field." Here, indeed, more fully than anywhere else, the traveller realizes the extent of the American exodus. At every turn, he meets members of the African race, single or in groups; he sees them building and painting houses, working in mills, engaged in every handicraft employment: here he notices a street occupied by colored shopkeepers and clerks: if he steps into the environs, he finds the blacks in every quarter, busy upon their gardens and farms.

The white population of Chatham is reckoned at four thousand: the number of colored persons in the town may be safely estimated at eight hundred. If to this estimate is added the number residing in the neighborhood, the total amount cannot be less than two thousand."[68]

Windsor, directly across the Detroit River from the city of Detroit, was home to about 1,400 people, with about 250 black residents. "The general appearances of these is very much in their favor. There are many good mechanics among them: nearly all have comfortable homes, and some occupy very neat and handsome houses of their own."[69]

Other towns with significant black populations included Sandwich, Buxton, and Camden. Farther to the east, some black refugees made their way to the provinces of Quebec, New Brunswick, and Nova Scotia.

Prejudice in Canada

Nineteenth-century Canadian law favored newcomers of any race. Black immigrants found it possible to purchase land at a relatively low cost. Fugitives were able to receive supplies and donations from abolitionists and

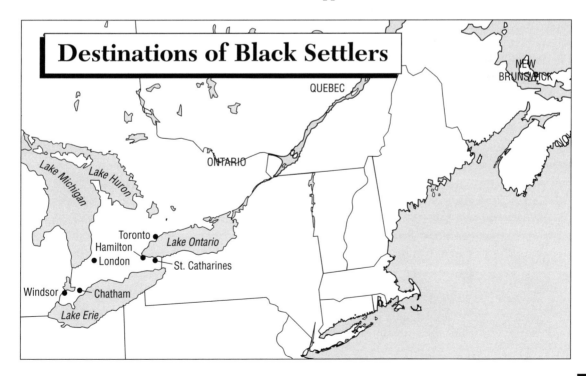

Destinations of Black Settlers

friends in the United States free from customs duty. Their children could attend local schools. Some blacks farmed their own plots of land, and since much of Canada was unsettled at that time, experienced farmhands were in great demand by white farmers who were clearing fields for the first time. Blacks who owned property were allowed to vote just as other immigrants were.

Despite these advantages, blacks in Canada still found themselves to be strangers in a strange land, and they faced the same sort of prejudice that they sought to escape in the United States. In 1863, J. W. Lindsay, born a slave in Tennessee, talked about discrimination in Canada:

I find the prejudice here the same as in the States. I don't find any difference at all. In fact, as far as prejudice goes, the slaveholders have not so much absolute prejudice as the people here—not half. . . . We may have the best [horse] teams in the world, and the best means in the world to carry on business, but unless we can make business [between] ourselves, such as gardening or something of that kind, we cannot get anything to do. Here are our children, that we think as much of as white people think of theirs; and want them elevated and educated; but, although I have been here thirty years, I have never seen a scholar made here amongst the colored people. I speak only of St. Catharines. There are several graduates in Toronto, I know. The Irish are getting so, down at the docks, where the colored men may do a few hours' work, once in a while, loading & unloading, that they want to run them off the docks. Then here are two railroads, and here is the canal, where there are about

Cold Canadian Weather

The first thing many slaves entering Canada noticed was an obvious change in climate. In the South, winters are mild and summers are hot and humid. In Canada, summers are short and cool and winters are cold, dark, and snowy; temperatures can easily dip to twenty degrees below zero in January. Samuel Ringgold Ward was born to slave parents in 1817. He escaped to the North and received a quality education in classics and theology. In his 1855 book, *Autobiography of a Fugitive Negro*, Ward describes what he saw crossing into Canada on a winter's day.

"It was a bitterly cold day, the 11th of January, 1853. Crossing the river, it was so cold that icicles were formed upon my clothes, as the waves dashed the water into the ferry boat. It was difficult for the Rev. H. Wilson and myself—we travelled together—to keep ourselves warm while driving; and my horses, at a most rapid rate, travelled twelve miles almost without sweating. That day, this poor fellow crossed that ferry with nothing upon his person but cotton clothing, and an oilcloth topcoat. Liberty was before him, and for it he could defy the frost. I had observed him, when I was in the office of the ferry, sitting not *at*, but *all around*, the stove; for he literally *surrounded and covered it* with his shivering legs and arms and trunk. And what delighted me was, everybody in the office seemed quite content that he should occupy what he had discovered and appropriated. I yielded my share without a word of complaint."

300 hands employed, and you won't see a colored face at either of them. The white folks won't give them any chance at all. I have asked the authorities here—"What are you going to do with the colored people? What will become of them? What kind of citizens will they make? You will only make paupers and culprits of them."[70]

Lewis Chambers, who was a black missionary in Canada, also encountered extreme bigotry:

The prejudice here against the colored people is stronger a great deal than it is in [Massachusetts]. Since I have been in the country, I went to a church one Sabbath, & the sexton asked me, "What do you want here to-day?" I said, "Is there not to be service here to-day?" He said, "Yes, but we don't want any niggers here." I said, "You are mistaken in the man. I am not a 'nigger', but a negro." Eight years ago, I was driven out of Wallaceburg, which is near Dresden, by a mob of lumbermen, simply because of my color, and there have been two or three colored men driven out of their houses, near Ridgetown. I built a new house three years ago, which was all paid for, and the day it was finished, some person put a match to it, and it was burned. It was not insured. There is [however] a good feeling towards colored people in Toronto and Montreal.[71]

Those Who Were Successful

As with any group of people, the stories of fugitive slaves who settled in Canada varied from person to person. People who suc-

Former slaves who were fortunate enough to live in supportive communities, were sometimes able to save money and become prosperous.

ceeded in the new land tended to come from border states where slaves were not treated as severely as those farther in the South. Those who were whipped, beaten, chained, and likewise traumatized carried deep psychological and emotional scars that conspired to prevent them from achieving all they might have under different circumstances.

In addition, there were the usual obstacles faced by any immigrant population trying to make new lives in a foreign land. Some were unlucky and met with prejudice; others found peace and security. The lives of the fugitives were shaped by varying degrees of providence, skill, determination, hardship, personal enterprise, and education. Those

Fugitives in Canada occasionally were able to save enough money to purchase their own property.

who settled in larger cities or predominantly black communities found less prejudice than those who moved to small towns and villages. Those whose neighbors were willing to work with them or buy their produce were able to save money and become prosperous. The stories of success gave hope to others in the United States who could foresee a better future north of the American border.

There were large tracts of rich land available to fugitives in Canada, and many ex-slaves had a strong desire to possess and cultivate their own farms. This desire drew many of them into the Canadian wilderness, where they were able to carve out little farms in the forest and live like pioneers.

In the 1840s, many black pioneers settled in an unsurveyed tract of land west of Toronto known as Queen's Bush. For years, there were no white people in this area. Black families farmed wheat on fifty- to one-hundred-acre tracts of land and made money by milling lumber cut from the trees in the nearby hardwood forests.

Aby B. Jones was a field hand in Madison County, Kentucky, until he was thirty years old. At that time he immigrated to Canada, where he was able to acquire some land. Jones had this to say about prospects for blacks in Canada:

I heard that in Canada colored men were free; therefore I came here, and am only sorry to say that I did not come years before I did.

When I came here I was not worth one cent. I neither begged nor received a farthing of money. I went to work at once, and, by the blessing of the Lord, I was prospered, and have placed my family beyond the reach of want.

I am satisfied, that any colored man coming to Canada, can, in a few years accumulate property to give himself and family a living.[72]

Of course, black people were successful in many enterprises besides farming. John H. Hill escaped to Toronto in 1853 and by hard work and determination was able to achieve wealth beyond his dreams. Hill wrote about his prosperous tobacco manufacturing business:

I don't see anything in the way of our doing a good business here. We employ twelve or fourteen hands now, and have white & black boys at work; there is such a demand for boys, that we have to take anybody we can get. There are four of us in the firm, all colored men. Our business is paying about $26 a day, and we hope to make it pay $50 a day. We mean to succeed. . . . When we came here, in 1855, we found no difficulty in getting [work in] the best shops of the city; and after we had worked here a while, I believe we were preferred, because we were steady & stuck to our work. I never heard of any objection being made to taking a colored boy into a shop to learn a trade. One of the best machinists in the city will take colored boys into his shop. There is no difficulty in a good colored mechanic getting work among white men. I think the

Levi Coffin Visits Canada

In 1844, Levi Coffin, who had helped thousands of fugitives escape to Canada, made a trip north to see how the ex-slaves were faring. Coffin joined forces with Isaac J. Rice, a white minister who had left the United States to open a mission in Canada for the poor, destitute runaways who still suffered the scars of slavery. Rice sheltered hundreds until other homes could be found, and his mission was the main "terminus," or landing point, for the Underground Railroad. Coffin and Rice traveled from town to town speaking to the new Canadian citizens. The following is an excerpt from *Reminiscences of Levi Coffin.*

"Here we had several meetings and visited many families, hearing thrilling stories of their narrow escapes, their great sufferings and the remarkable providences that attended their efforts to gain freedom. They told how they had prayed to the Lord, asking him to be with them and protect them in their flight from their tyrannical masters, and how he had never forsaken them in their time of need, but had fulfilled his promise to go with them. They frequently spoke as if they had held personal conversations with the Lord, and their simple and untutored language was full of expression of praise and thanksgiving. I was often led to believe that these poor . . . and degraded sons and daughters of Africa, who were not able to read the words of the precious Savior, were blessed with a clearer, plainer manifestation of the Holy Spirit than many of us who have had better opportunities of cultivation. My heart was often touched and my eyes filled with tears on hearing their simple stories."

colored people, after a while, will surmount the prejudice against them.[73]

Building Schools and Settlements

Since it was illegal in the United States to teach slaves to read and write, those who escaped into Canada understood the necessity of getting an education for themselves and their children. Under Canadian law, black people were permitted to send their children to public schools. Unfortunately, the laws were not strictly enforced, and blacks were not readily admitted to white schools in Canada. Canadian law also allowed blacks to set up separate schools from a portion of their share of government school funds. In some districts, however, prejudice stood in the way of black education. Schools in the towns of Sandwich, Chatham, London, and Hamilton were tainted with discrimination. Benjamin Drew writes in *A North-Side View of Slavery,*

> The principal reason for this . . . [is] the whites objected to having their children sit in the same [rows] with the colored pupils; and some of the [people of the] lower classes will not send their children to schools where the blacks are admitted. Under these circumstances, it is unpleasant to the colored children to attend public schools—especially if any of the teachers happen to be victims of the very prejudice which they should induce others to overcome.[74]

Some blacks confronted the prejudice, however, and after years of complaining to government officials found that their school situations had improved. William Thompson, the second black person to move to the town of Galt, remembered,

> When I came here, colored children were not received into schools. I fought, and fought, and fought, and at last it got to the governor, and the law was declared, that all had equal rights.[75]

Other problems conspired to prevent black children from receiving a proper education. Some immigrants were too poor to take advantage of schooling opportunities and needed their children to work to help support the family. Others who were unaccustomed to equal rights with whites were too timid to ask for them. And there was the cold Canadian climate. As Wilbur Siebert wrote, "The children, unused to the climate of the new country, perhaps also thinly clad, were sickly and often unable to go to school."[76]

To overcome these problems, at least at a local level, abolitionist Quakers in England donated $1,500 to black reverends Josiah Henson and Hiram Wilson to set up a school near the town of Dresden in Canada West. The Dawn Institute, as it was called, was to teach basic academics as well as "mechanical arts" to boys and "domestic arts" to girls. To further those goals, the Dawn Institute purchased three hundred acres on the Big Bear River. Fugitive slaves who heard of the school moved to the area and built homes on institute land.

The area where the institute was built was forested with valuable black walnut trees. Reverend Henson set up a sawmill so that the settlers could support themselves selling the lumber while their children went to school. At its inception, the school taught fourteen students, from among fifty blacks living on institute land. By 1852, that number had grown to sixty students, and the settlers on the land had increased to five hundred. At

Liberia

In 1822, the U.S. government and a private organization called the American Colonization Society launched an experimental campaign to resettle freed slaves in Africa. Working with abolitionists and black organizations, the plan was to set up a free black country in the region of Africa that had been most seriously affected by the transatlantic slave trade, which was coming to an end around that time. The black settlers established several separate settlements over the next few decades. In all, 2,638 American blacks migrated to the region. In 1847 the settlements were united to form the country of Liberia on the western bulge of the African continent.

The American Colonization Society, organized on December 28, 1816, was supported by many clergy as well as some leading free blacks who believed that blacks would never receive just treatment in America. Most free blacks opposed the resettlement plan, however, because they believed the motives of the organization's leaders were strictly racist: The Colonization Society wanted free blacks removed from the South so that they could not aid in the escape of their enslaved brothers and sisters. The society continued its efforts well into the twentieth century, but it was never successful in convincing many African Americans to return to the continent of their ancestors.

Liberia itself faced many problems, including conflicts between westernized blacks from the United States and the region's indigenous African inhabitants, and it remained a poor country with many political and social problems.

---

this time, the classrooms of the Dawn Institute were opened to local white and Indian children as well.

Several other similar schools were set up in Canada. In the 1850s, Henry Bibb, a fugitive slave who was active in the abolition movement, set up a colony in Canada called the Refugees' Home. Bibb sold twenty-five-acre lots to settlers, who built log cabins and cleared the land to raise crops and vegetables. In 1852, a Quaker named Laura S. Haviland began the first school at the Refugees' Home. Haviland found that many of her students were able to read and write after only six weeks of tutoring.

Near the shores of Lake Erie, a mission of the Presbyterian Church founded the Elgin Settlement and a town called Buxton. Families that entered the settlement could purchase fifty-acre farms at a cost of $2.50 per acre, payable in monthly installments. By 1862, Buxton had grown to over one thousand black people. A day school and a Sunday school provided instruction to the children of the settlers. According to Dr. Samuel Howe, who wrote a valuable report on the life of fugitive settlers in Canada,

Buxton is certainly an interesting place. Sixteen years ago it was a wilderness. Now, good highways are laid out in all directions through the forest; and by their side, standing back thirty-three feet from the road, are about two hundred cottages, all built on the same pattern, all looking neat and comfortable. Around each one is a cleared place, of several acres, which is well cultivated. The fences are in good order, the barns seem well-filled; and cattle and horses, and pigs and poultry, abound. There are signs of industry and thrift and comfort everywhere; signs of intemperance, of idleness, of want, nowhere. There is no tavern, and no groggery; but there is a chapel and a schoolhouse.

Most interesting of all are the inhabitants. Twenty years ago most of them were slaves, who owned nothing, not even their children. Now they own themselves; they own their houses and farms; and they have their wives and children about them. They are enfranchised citizens of a government which protects their rights. . . . The present condition of all these colonists, as compared with their former one is very remarkable. . . . This settlement is a perfect success. . . . Here are men who were bred in slavery, who came here and purchased land at the government prices, cleared it, bought their own implements, built their own houses after a model, and have supported themselves in all material circumstances, and now support their schools.[77]

Although Canada offered a place of safety to the ex-slaves, when slavery was abolished after the Civil War, many blacks returned to the United States. Whether it was the cold Canadian climate or the desire to reunite with friends and family who had been left behind, the black communities in Canada shrunk after the Civil War. For those who stayed, however, Canada remained a place where opportunity and success could be found if one possessed luck and was willing to work for his or her dreams in a new land.

Fighting New Battles

The battle over slavery had threatened to destroy the United States for decades. In the first half of the nineteenth century, the United States was a growing country. Every time a new state was added to the Union, political conflicts erupted over whether the state would be a slave state or a free state. The Fugitive Slave Law of 1850 was actually passed to appease southern senators who were worried when California was admitted to the Union as a free state. But many congressmen were not happy with this compromise and threatened to leave, or secede, from the Union unless the Fugitive Slave Law was strictly enforced.

Hostilities between the North and South continued unabated. It seemed to most Americans that there simply could not be any compromise between those who believed in slavery and those who did not. When antislavery president Abraham Lincoln was elected in 1860, South Carolina seceded from the Union. It was quickly followed by Alabama, Florida, Georgia, Louisiana, Mississippi, and Texas. These states formed their own country, called the Confederate States of America. When the Confederates seized Fort Sumter in South Carolina on April 14, 1861, the Civil War began.

The war raged for four bloody years, with hundreds of thousands of American men wounded or killed in battle. By the time it was over on April 9, 1865, the South lay in ruins, and 600,000 Americans lay dead. In December of the same year, the Thirteenth Amendment to the Constitution was ratified, legally abolishing slavery in the United States.

Escaped Slaves Help Fight the Civil War

During the Civil War, more than 200,000 blacks deserted the plantations to join the Union army. Although they initially did only menial jobs, black soldiers eventually fought in several important battles. In fact, some military historians maintain that without this influx of soldiers, the North might not have

Arguments over slavery between the North and the South sometimes erupted in violence.

More than 200,000 blacks fled southern plantations to join the Union effort during the Civil War.

been able to mount a successful military initiative to win the war. In 1935, black civil rights leader W. E. B. DuBois explained how African Americans helped the North win the Civil War:

> Freedom for the slave was the logical result of a crazy attempt [by the South] to wage war in the midst of four million black slaves, and trying the while . . . to ignore the interests of those slaves in the outcome of the fighting. Yet, these slaves had enormous power in their hands. Simply by stopping work, they could threaten the Confederacy with starvation. By walking into the Federal camps, they showed to doubting Northerners the easy possibility of using them thus, but by the same gesture, depriving their enemies of their use in just these fields. It was the fugitive slave who made the slaveholders face the alternative of surrendering to the North, or to the Negroes.
>
> It was this plain alternative that brought [Confederate general Robert E.] Lee's

sudden surrender. Either the South must make terms with its slaves, free them, use them to fight the North, and thereafter no longer treat them as bondsmen; or they could surrender to the North with the assumption that the North after the war, must help them to defend slavery, as it had before.[78]

Reconstruction

Although the South was destroyed by the Civil War, little was changed for the black people who remained. Owners of plantations that were not destroyed once again made African Americans work in the fields with little or no monetary compensation. Southern states replaced slave codes with "black codes" that gave ex-slaves some basic rights but still discriminated against them. Blacks were forbidden to testify in court. In many states blacks were forbidden to own guns and meet in unsupervised groups. Former slave owners made black workers sign strict labor contracts making the former slaves liable to criminal penalties if the contracts were not fulfilled. Stiff, discriminatory laws were passed, and black children were forced into so-called apprenticeships that guaranteed their virtual slavery to whites.

Meanwhile, the government set up the Freedman's Bureau to help resettled black and white Civil War refugees. Run by the U.S. Army, the bureau provided homes and jobs for former slaves as well as medicine and health care. The bureau built more than 4,000 schools, which eventually educated 250,000 black Americans.

The widespread passage of black codes forced the federal government to act. In 1867, Congress passed the Reconstruction Act, which put ten southern states under martial law. Congress also passed the Fourteenth Amendment to the Constitution, which guaranteed every person equal rights under the law regardless of race.

In 1870, the Fifteenth Amendment to the Constitution guaranteed black men the right to vote. (Women would not be allowed to vote until 1920.) Since African Americans made up the majority of many southern congressional districts, the new governments they elected were the most progressive the region had ever seen. Since Lincoln had been a Republican, black voters almost unanimously voted for Republicans who advocated free public schools, reformed labor laws to make them more fair to employees, and eliminated laws that discriminated against blacks. Legislatures also abolished common criminal punishments such as whipping and branding.

For the first time, blacks were elected to state and federal governments. Mississippi sent three black men to the U.S. Congress; South Carolina sent two. By 1900, twenty black men had served in Congress. Blacks were also elected to city governments, as judges, and to other posts.

Many southern whites were violently opposed to the gains made by former slaves. Civil War veterans formed secret organizations

Black men line up to vote after gaining the right in 1870.

to terrorize black people and prevent them from exercising their rights. The groups had names such as the White Brotherhood, the Rifle Clubs, the Palefaces, and the Ku Klux Klan. Klan members dressed in hoods and white sheets that were supposed to make them look like dead Confederate soldiers who had risen from the grave. Members used whips, guns, and lynchings to kill innocent African American men, women, and children. Black homes, schools, and farms were burned to the ground.

Reconstruction officially ended in 1877 when federal troops left the South. Once again blacks were left to fend for themselves in a hostile territory. Powerful white leaders quickly negated the gains made by blacks. Election days were marked by terrorist acts by the Klan that prevented African Americans from going to the polls. By 1901, all of the black members of Congress had been voted out of office.

The south passed so-called Jim Crow laws that enforced black segregation. The laws got their name from a practice of the early 1800s. Since black actors at that time were not allowed to perform in theaters attended by whites, white actors performed in blackface makeup. In 1831, a white singer painted his face black and sang a song called "Jump, Jim

An 1885 woodcut depicts the tortures inflicted on blacks by members of the Ku Klux Klan.

Life on the Underground Railroad

The Jim Crow laws, which segregated blacks, were enforced in some southern states until the 1960s.

Crow." That song quickly became associated with segregation.

Jim Crow laws prevented African Americans from using public transportation and from going to theaters, restaurants, and other public places. Laws charging "poll taxes" were also passed. Laws requiring black people who wanted to vote to pass incomprehensible civic tests that asked such questions as the exact wording of an obscure clause in the Constitution also acted as a deterrent to black voting. The unjust Jim Crow laws remained strictly enforced in the southern states until the 1950s and the 1960s.

The Underground Railroad Today

While the Underground Railroad was revered for the help it provided to fugitive slaves, most estimates state that the railroad helped at most 100,000 people out of more than 3 million who were held as slaves. Although most slaves were not directly helped by the railroad, some historians believe that if there had never been an underground railroad, there would have never been a Civil War, be-

cause the greatest friction between the northern and southern states was the aid given to runaways. And without the Civil War, it might have been many more years before the inhuman system of slavery was abolished in the United States.

The United States is one of the most wealthy and powerful countries in the world. Much of that power was built in the eighteenth and nineteenth centuries by the blood, sweat, and toil of African American slaves. But a country is made up of more than money and power. As Frederick Douglass wrote, a country also has a spiritual obligation to its people.

It is the soul that makes a nation great or small, noble or ignoble, weak or strong. It is the soul that exalts it to happiness or sinks it to misery. . . . It is the spiritual side of humanity. Though occult and impalpable, it is as real as iron. The laws of its life are spiritual, not [of the flesh], and it must conform to these laws or it starves and dies. . . . The life of the nation is secure only while the nation is honest, truthful, and virtuous, for upon these conditions depends the life of its life.[79]

Fighting New Battles **83**

Notes

Introduction: The Long Road to Freedom

1. Quoted in Henrietta Buckmaster, *Let My People Go*. 1941. Reprint, Boston: Beacon Press, 1966, p. 19.
2. Quoted in Wilbur H. Siebert, *The Underground Railroad from Slavery to Freedom*. 1898. Reprint, New York: Russell & Russell, 1967, p. 20.
3. Quoted in Siebert, *The Underground Railroad from Slavery to Freedom*, p. 48.
4. Siebert, *The Underground Railroad from Slavery to Freedom*, p. 28.
5. William Breyfogle, *Make Free*. Philadelphia: J. B. Lippincott, 1958, p. 16.

Chapter 1: A Slave's Life

6. Kenneth M. Stampp, *The Peculiar Institution*. 1956. Reprint, New York: Knopf, 1978, p. 246.
7. Quoted in Charles L. Perdue Jr., Thomas E. Barden, and Robert K. Phillips, eds., *Weevils in the Wheat*. Charlottesville: University of Virginia Press, 1992, p. 94.
8. Quoted in Stampp, *The Peculiar Institution*, p. 197.
9. Frederick Douglass, *Narrative of the Life of Frederick Douglass: An American Slave*. 1845. Reprint, New York: Penguin Books, 1982, p. 48.
10. Quoted in Perdue, Barden, and Phillips, *Weevils in the Wheat*, pp. 223–24.
11. Quoted in Stampp, *The Peculiar Institution*, p. 40.
12. Quoted in Perdue, Barden, and Phillips, *Weevils in the Wheat*, p. 152.
13. Stampp, *The Peculiar Institution*, p. 61.
14. Joe Gray Taylor, *Negro Slavery in Louisiana*. Baton Rouge: Louisiana Historical Association, 1963, p. 62.
15. Quoted in Taylor, *Negro Slavery in Louisiana*, pp. 68–69.
16. Quoted in Perdue, Barden, and Phillips, *Weevils in the Wheat*, p. 202.
17. Quoted in Perdue, Barden, and Phillips, *Weevils in the Wheat*, p. 105.
18. Quoted in Ralph Betts Flanders, *Plantation Slavery in Georgia*. 1933. Reprint, Cos Cob, CT: John E. Edwards, 1967, p. 154.
19. Quoted in Flanders, *Plantation Slavery in Georgia*, p. 155.
20. Quoted in Perdue, Barden, and Phillips, *Weevils in the Wheat*, p. 181.
21. Quoted in Perdue, Barden, and Phillips, *Weevils in the Wheat*, p. 81.
22. Quoted in Perdue, Barden, and Phillips, *Weevils in the Wheat*, p. 57.

Chapter 2: Life on the Run

23. Quoted in Ulrich Phillips, ed., *Plantation and Frontier, 1649–1863*, vol. 2. New York: B. Franklin, 1969, p. 108.
24. Frederick Douglass, *My Bondage and My Freedom*. 1855. Reprint, New York: Arno Press, 1968, pp. 263–64.
25. Quoted in Stampp, *The Peculiar Institution*, p. 90.
26. Douglass, *My Bondage and My Freedom*, pp. 282–84.
27. Quoted in George P. Rawick, *From Sundown to Sunup: The Making of the Black Community*. Westport, CT: Greenwood, 1972, p. 103.

28. William Still, *The Underground Rail Road*. 1872. Reprint, Chicago: Johnson, 1970, p. 38.

29. Quoted in John F. Bayliss, ed., *Black Slave Narratives*. New York: Macmillan, 1970, pp. 192–94.

30. Quoted in John W. Blassingame, ed., *Slave Testimony*. Baton Rouge: Louisiana State University Press, 1995, p. 305.

31. Quoted in Blassingame, *Slave Testimony*, pp. 518–19.

32. Quoted in Blassingame, *Slave Testimony*, p. 521.

33. Quoted in Still, *The Underground Rail Road*, p. 155.

Chapter 3: Lives of the Trackers

34. Quoted in Stampp, *The Peculiar Institution*, p. 153.

35. James Curtis Ballagh, *A History of Slavery in Virginia*. 1902. Reprint, Johnson Reprint Corporation, 1968, p. 91.

36. Breyfogle, *Make Free*, p. 215.

37. Douglass, *Narrative of the Life of Frederick Douglass*, pp. 143–44.

38. Breyfogle, *Make Free*, pp. 215–16.

39. Still, *The Underground Rail Road*, pp. 116–17.

40. Breyfogle, *Make Free*, pp. 216–17.

41. Quoted in Stampp, *The Peculiar Institution*, p. 188.

42. Quoted in Blassingame, *Slave Testimony*, p. 280.

43. Quoted in Blassingame, *Slave Testimony*, pp. 222–23.

44. Quoted in Stampp, *The Peculiar Institution*, p. 213.

Chapter 4: Lives of the Conductors

45. Buckmaster, *Let My People Go*, p. 29.

46. Breyfogle, *Make Free*, pp. 23–24.

47. Siebert, *The Underground Railroad from Slavery to Freedom*, p. 87.

48. Siebert, *The Underground Railroad from Slavery to Freedom*, p. 65.

49. Levi Coffin, *Reminiscences of Levi Coffin*. 1876. Reprint, New York: Arno Press, 1968, p. 317.

50. Quoted in Blassingame, *Slave Testimony*, p. 520.

51. Sarah Bradford, *Harriet Tubman: The Moses of Her People*. 1869. Reprint, Gloucester, MA: Peter Smith, 1981, p. 55.

52. Bradford, *Harriet Tubman*, p. 33.

53. Siebert, *The Underground Railroad from Slavery to Freedom*, pp. 87–88.

Chapter 5: Stations and Stationmasters

54. Siebert, *The Underground Railroad from Slavery to Freedom*, p. 49.

55. Coffin, *Reminiscences of Levi Coffin*, pp. 108–109.

56. Quoted in Siebert, *The Underground Railroad from Slavery to Freedom*, p. 52.

57. Coffin, *Reminiscences of Levi Coffin*, pp. 112–13.

58. Coffin, *Reminiscences of Levi Coffin*, p. 301.

59. Breyfogle, *Make Free*, p. 178.

60. Buckmaster, *Let My People Go*, p. 151.

61. Buckmaster, *Let My People Go*, p. 152.

Chapter 6: Building New Lives in Canada

62. Horatio T. Strother, *The Underground Railroad in Connecticut*. Middletown, CT: Wesleyan University Press, 1962, p. 8.

63. Benjamin Drew, *A North-Side View of Slavery*. 1856. Reprint, New York: Johnson Reprint Corporation, 1968, p. 18.

64. Drew, *A North-Side View of Slavery*, p. 17.
65. Drew, *A North-Side View of Slavery*, pp. 94–95.
66. Quoted in Drew, *A North-Side View of Slavery*, p. 136.
67. Drew, *A North-Side View of Slavery*, p. 147.
68. Drew, *A North-Side View of Slavery*, p. 234.
69. Drew, *A North-Side View of Slavery*, p. 321.
70. Quoted in Blassingame, *Slave Testimony*, p. 397.
71. Quoted in Blassingame, *Slave Testimony*, pp. 413–14.
72. Quoted in Drew, *A North-Side View of Slavery*, p. 150.
73. Quoted in Blassingame, *Slave Testimony*, pp. 428–29.
74. Drew, *A North-Side View of Slavery*, p. 147.
75. Quoted in Drew, *A North-Side View of Slavery*, p. 137.
76. Siebert, *The Underground Railroad from Slavery to Freedom*, p. 229.
77. Quoted in Siebert, *The Underground Railroad from Slavery to Freedom*, pp. 208–209.

Epilogue: Fighting New Battles

78. Quoted in Rawick, *From Sundown to Sunup*, p. 97.
79. Frederick Douglass, *The Mind and Heart of Frederick Douglass*. New York: Thomas Y. Crowell, 1968, pp. 194–95.

For Further Reading

Sarah Bradford, *Harriet Tubman: The Moses of Her People*. 1869. Reprint, Gloucester, MA: Peter Smith, 1981. First published when Harriet Tubman was still alive, this book is the biography of the most famous conductor on the Underground Railroad. It contains vivid details of her struggles as a slave in Maryland and her heroic actions while leading slaves to freedom.

William Breyfogle, *Make Free*. Philadelphia: J. B. Lippincott, 1958. Breyfogle was a Rhodes scholar at Oxford who re-created the facts about the Underground Railroad in a thrilling narrative full of personalities and stories that make history come alive.

Levi Coffin, *Reminiscences of Levi Coffin*. 1876. Reprint, New York: Arno Press, 1968. First published when Coffin was seventy-eight years old, this book has become an indispensable primary resource on the Underground Railroad. Coffin wrote from a wealth of experience, having helped nearly three thousand runaway slaves in their escape.

Frederick Douglass, *The Mind and Heart of Frederick Douglass*. New York: Thomas Y. Crowell, 1968. This book is a collection of speeches given by one of the most famous slave refugees after he became America's premier orator by speaking out for abolition. Douglass's pronouncements on racism, slavery, and other topics still ring true.

———, *My Bondage and My Freedom*. 1845. Reprint, New York: Arno Press, 1968. This book is the autobiography detailing the hideous institutions of slavery in a poetic and emotionally charged language.

———, *Narrative of the Life of Frederick Douglass: An American Slave*. 1845. Reprint, New York: Penguin Books, 1982. Published in 1845, this autobiography of Frederick Douglass powerfully details the life of the internationally famous abolitionist from his birth in 1818 to his escape North in 1838. Douglass writes about how he endured physical and mental brutality, how he learned to read and write, and how he stepped forward to lead the dangerous and frustrating crusade against slavery.

James Haskins, *Get on Board*. New York: Scholastic, 1993. A young adult book written by a professor of English at the University of Florida that contains detailed stories about those who escaped slavery and those who helped them.

Stephan R. Lilley, *Fighters Against American Slavery*. San Diego: Lucent Books, 1999. A book from the "History Makers" series that details the lives of famous abolitionists and other antislave personalities, including William Lloyd Garrison, Frederick Douglass, John Brown, and others.

Charles L. Perdue Jr., Thomas E. Barden, and Robert K. Phillips, eds., *Weevils in the Wheat*. Charlottesville: University of Virginia Press, 1992. In 1936, the all-Negro unit of the Virginia Writers' Project began interviewing ex-slaves who were still alive in Virginia. The stories of more than three hundred elderly African Americans were written down and compiled in this easy-to-read and insightful book about the day-to-day lives of slaves.

Kem Knapp Sawyer, *The Underground Railroad in American History*. Springfield, NJ: Enslow, 1997. A young adult book that details the intense determination of those who worked on the Underground Railroad.

Works Consulted

James Curtis Ballagh, *A History of Slavery in Virginia*. 1902. Reprint, New York: Johnson Reprint Corporation, 1968. This book gives all the facts and details about the nearly 250-year-old institution of slavery in the state of Virginia.

John F. Bayliss, ed., *Black Slave Narratives*. New York: Macmillan, 1970. Fascinating and authentic stories of slaves who worked on the plantations and farms of the American South. Chapters detail slaves' former lives in Africa, relations between masters and slaves, slaveholder brutality, family life, and more.

John W. Blassingame, ed., *Slave Testimony*. Baton Rouge: Louisiana State University Press, 1995. More than seven hundred pages of letters, speeches, interviews, and autobiographies of men and women who were slaves over the course of two centuries.

Charles L. Blockson, *Hippocrene Guide to the Underground Railroad*. New York: Hippocrene Books, 1994. Blockson is the chairman of the advisory committee to the National Park Service who conducted a study of historic Underground Railroad sites still in existence. The book is a travel guide that lists more than two hundred existing landmark houses, institutions, buildings, and markers relating to the Underground Railroad.

Henrietta Buckmaster, *Let My People Go*. 1941. Reprint, Boston: Beacon Press, 1966. Buckmaster was a Quaker who wrote about the Underground Railroad, the abolition movement, and black struggles against racism, as well as women's history.

Benjamin Drew, *A North-Side View of Slavery*. 1856. Reprint, New York: Johnson Reprint Corporation, 1968. This book is an account of the history and condition of the fugitive slaves living in Canada as told in their own words.

Ralph Betts Flanders, *Plantation Slavery in Georgia*. 1933. Reprint, Cos Cob, CT: John E. Edwards, 1967. Written during the Great Depression, this book offers details of slavery as well as the economics of plantation agriculture in the eighteenth and nineteenth centuries.

H. U. Johnson, *From Dixie to Canada: Romances and Realities of the Underground Railroad*. Orwell, OH: H. U. Johnson, 1896. Describes in vivid detail the individual stories of more than a dozen men and women who escaped to Canada on the Underground Railroad.

Ulrich Phillips, ed., *Plantation and Frontier, 1649–1863*. Vol. 2. New York: B. Franklin, 1969. A collection of source essays concerning the expansion of America through the agricultural, economic, and social control.

George P. Rawick, *From Sundown to Sunup: The Making of the Black Community*. Westport, CT: Greenwood, 1972. Written by an associate professor of sociology at Washington University in St. Louis, this book analyzes the effects of slavery on African American culture in the twentieth century.

Wilbur H. Siebert, *The Underground Railroad from Slavery to Freedom*. 1898. Reprint, New York: Russell & Russell, 1967. Siebert was an associate professor of history at Ohio State University in the

1890s, and this book is a definitive resource that was written when records of the Underground Railroad were still relatively fresh.

Kenneth M. Stampp, *The Peculiar Institution.* 1956. Reprint, New York: Knopf, 1978. Written by a professor of American history at the University of California, Berkeley, this book is a definitive source on every aspect of slavery in the United States, including how the slaves worked, how they resisted bondage, how they behaved toward their masters, how they developed their own culture, and other themes.

William Still, *The Underground Rail Road.* 1872. Reprint, Chicago: Johnson, 1970. This book contains more than eight hundred pages that detail the stories of escaped slaves and the lives of those who tried to help them. Still's records are among the few that were hidden, rather than destroyed, after the passage of the Fugitive Slave Law of 1850.

Horatio T. Strother, *The Underground Railroad in Connecticut.* Middletown, CT: Wesleyen University Press, 1962. Although the focus of this book is the work of Underground Railroad activities in the state of Connecticut, it also details fascinating accounts of the *Amistad* slave ship trial and other New England antislavery operations.

Joe Gray Taylor, *Negro Slavery in Louisiana.* Baton Rouge: Louisiana Historical Association, 1963. A view of slavery on Louisiana's sugar and cotton plantations.

Samuel Ringgold Ward, *Autobiography of a Fugitive Negro.* 1855. Reprint, New York: Arno Press and the New York Times, 1968. The author of this book was a gifted black orator whose parents escaped slavery and fled to New York. Ward was educated in classics and theology and was a pastor in New York State and Indiana, where his congregation was entirely white. In flowery language, this book describes Ward's travels in the United States, Canada, and Great Britain while he was working for the abolition of slavery.

Index

Picture Credits

Cover photo: Peter Newark's American Pictures
Archive Photos: 10, 24, 62
Corbis, 63
Corbis/Bettmann, 12, 13, 17, 22, 23, 26, 39, 43, 44, 47, 54, 61, 80, 82
Courtesy Stuart A. Kallen, 50

Library of Congress, 9, 18, 40, 68, 69, 83
National Archives, 30
North Wind Picture Archives, 11, 15, 19, 20, 25, 27, 28, 35, 37, 49, 53, 55, 57, 58, 65, 73, 74, 79
Stock Montage, Inc., 14, 32, 33, 34, 42, 48, 59

About the Author

Stuart A. Kallen is the author of more than 145 nonfiction books for children and young adults. He has written on topics ranging from the theory of relativity to rock and roll history to life on the American frontier. In addition, Mr. Kallen has written award-winning children's videos and television scripts. In the 1970s, Mr. Kallen lived in a house that had been a station on the Underground Railroad. The house was a former inn built in 1803 in Millfield, Ohio, and contained several rumored ghosts, along with two secret rooms accessible only from a trapdoor in the attic.